"This fine collection of reflections on Christian spirituality in the context of academia gives voice to an impressively diverse group of professors from a variety of scholarly disciplines and churchly traditions. Their reflections provide insightful commentary and observations on the spiritual implications of the 'learning experience,' a potential two-way street between faculty and students alike."

—**Bill J. Leonard,** Professor of Divinity Emeritus, Founding Dean, School of Divinity, Wake Forest University

"John Dunaway and I have been not-too-distant neighbors since I moved in 1987 from the University of California at Berkeley to the University of Georgia. Athens, Georgia is about 90 miles northeast of Macon, where John taught for his entire distinguished academic career at Mercer University. I knew John as the spokesman and unofficial leader of Christian faculty at Mercer. He would from time to time drive up to Athens to share insights with the Christian faculty group here. I strongly recommend his new book, *Minding Our Hearts.* The book is a collection of devotional vignettes written by Christian faculty from several universities. The authors I know personally include John, Russ Carlson, Phil Bishop, and Rae Mellichamp, all leaders on their campuses. The book is a long jump from Dunaway's usual intellectual writings on modern French religious writers, but the result is equally valuable and more approachable for nerd scientists like me. Bravo, John!"

—**Henry F. Schaefer III,** Graham Perdue Professor of Chemistry; Director, Center for Computational Quantum Chemistry, University of Georgia

"What a wonderful and needed volume for Christian professors. So often we exist untethered to a community of other believing scholars, often feeling like we are facing challenges alone. This book of devotionals, designed to provide one a week over the course of a year, will not only link you to other Christian professors but will also focus and refocus you in your calling, serving God through the life of the mind and heart. Be blessed!"

—**Michael O. Emerson,** Professor and Research Fellow in Religion and Public Policy, Baker Institute for Public Policy, Rice University

Minding Our Hearts

Minding Our Hearts

Devotionals on the Teaching Life for Christian Professors

John Marson Dunaway, Editor

Integratio Press
Pasco, Washington

MINDING OUR HEARTS: Devotionals on the Teaching Life for
Christian Professors

This is a publication of Axios, a Division of Integratio Press.

integratiopress.com

Integratio Press is an Imprint of the Christianity and Communication
Studies Network.
11503 Easton Dr.
Pasco, WA 99301

www.theccsn.com

Cover Design: Carol O'Callaghan
Interior Design: Carol O'Callaghan
Cover Image: Cloister of Cadouin Abbey, France. November 23, 2024. Used
with permission.

paperback isbn: 978-1-959685-35-7
ebook isbn: 978-1-959685-36-4

Library of Congress Control Number available from the publisher.

For my wife, Trish,
who conceived the vision of this book
and was a constant helper, indeed "meet."[1]

Table of Contents

Acknowledgements

I first must thank all the contributors to this volume. I had a list of colleagues both at my home institution of Mercer University and at colleges all over the United States and abroad. However, the more people I contacted, the wider the networking has spread. I now have a number of new colleagues far beyond those I had met through professional organizations and conferences, and for that expanded network of colleagues I am deeply grateful. It is a great encouragement to discover sisters and brothers in Christ in academic institutions, both church-related and public, who are committed to serving their Savior on a university campus. One of my new contacts even introduced me to our publisher. These new connections have reinforced my gratitude for the reality of the Communion of the Saints.

Bill Hager, a semi-retired Faculty Commons staffer, has been a dear friend and advisor for close to three decades, and he has been a frequent resource. His editing of the "Missional Moments" weekly devotionals, which are emailed to over 2,000 Christian professors worldwide, has provided spiritual food and encouragement to Christian faculty members for years.[2] I have leaned heavily on his advice.

Rick Hove, executive director of Faculty Commons, the faculty ministry of Cru, has also been a ready resource.[3]

Robert H. Woods Jr. at Integratio Press has been the ideal editor. Flexible, accessible, full of creative ideas, and devoted to making this book a valuable resource for Christian faculty members, he has become a friend and brother, despite our never having bridged the entire continent of North America that separates us.

Finally, I must mention Walter Bradley (longtime professor at Texas A & M and Baylor University), who passed away while this book was being written, and Rae Mellichamp (University of Alabama), who were the visionary builders of Christian faculty ministries, starting as far back as the 1970s.

Foreword

When you meet John Dunaway, the first thing you notice is that his eyes are smiling at you. Then you realize that it's not just his eyes, but his whole face is smiling. And if a body has a language, John's body language is that of joy. Having known John for over thirty years, I've determined that the joy that emanates from him has its source in John's deep and abiding relationship with Jesus. His heart overflows out of him onto other people because his heart is united with Christ.

So, I'm not surprised that a devotional book that John has conceived is about the heart. After all, isn't the heart what life is all about?

But John is also a world class scholar. He has spent decades in academia, developing the life of the mind in himself and in multitudes of his students. So I'm also not surprised that John would birth a devotional book to fully engage the mind. After all, isn't the mind what academia is all about?

This devotional book, engaging both the heart and the mind, is uniquely for Christian professors. More specifically, this book is for Christians that happen to be professors, not professors who happen to be Christians. Those who are Christians first and foremost will be encouraged, motivated, and challenged by these devotionals. They will need it.

Christian faculty, particularly those in secular institutions, not only carry the burdens of their nonbelieving colleagues of research, teaching, and service, but they also have hearts that burn for the salvation of their students and minds that ache to represent well a biblical worldview. They take seriously the intercession from the Lord's prayer that "Thy will be done on earth as it is in heaven." Serious nourishment is needed for those who labor in such a difficult field.

Several years ago, John asked me to speak to the Christian faculty group that he facilitated at Mercer University. Since the meeting was during lunch hour, John said that he would provide my lunch. After the meeting was over and all the other faculty had left to attend to their professorial duties, John and I sat down at the table to enjoy our lunch. John handed me a brown paper bag and kept another one for himself. Each bag contained a sandwich, a bag of chips, and an apple. As we chit-chatted about the meeting, I bit into the best sandwich I had ever tasted. Fresh bakery bread, slices of thinly carved ham, Swiss cheese, iceberg lettuce, Dijon mustard, and a crisp dill pickle slice had my taste buds singing the Hallelujah chorus. Now it's your turn. In this devotional, John is inviting you to sit down and taste and see that the Lord is good. He has served up food for the heart and the mind. Bon Appétit.

— **Bill Hager**, Editor, "Missional Moments," a weekly online devotional

List of Contributors

William F. Bina is Professor and Dean Emeritus at Mercer University School of Medicine. An alumnus of the United States Naval Academy who served on a nuclear submarine, his Doctor of Medicine degree is from the University of Nebraska College of Medicine.

Phillip Bishop is Professor Emeritus of Exercise Science at the University of Alabama. He has authored two books and over 200-refereed science publications and mentored 52 PhD students as dissertation chair. Phil and his wife Brenda are now Affiliate staff with Faculty Commons.

Russell Carlson is Emeritus Professor of Biochemistry and Molecular Biology in the Complex Carbohydrate Research Center at the University of Georgia. He and his wife Cheryl reside in Athens, Georgia and have been blessed with 56 years of marriage, 6 children, and 10 grandchildren.

Paul Chen teaches courses primarily on law in the Political Science Department at Western Washington University. He has published articles on Supreme Court decision-making, interest group litigation, and U.S. constitutional federalism. He sums up his worldview in three words: "*Everything* is connected."

Andy D. Digh, a lifelong Baptist nurtured in North Carolina, has faithfully served the students of Mercer University as a teacher and advisor since 1998. His vocational calling to education has served as a cornerstone of his faith, providing him with a profound sense of purpose and assurance.

The late **E. Jane Doering** was Professor of French literature and culture at Notre Dame University. She was an accomplished scholar on the works of Simone Weil, as well as a fondly remembered friend and colleague.

John Marson Dunaway is Professor Emeritus of French and Interdisciplinary Studies at Mercer University in Macon, Georgia, where he also served as Director of the Mercer Commons, a Center for Faith, Learning, and Vocation. He writes primarily on French religious writers.

Geri Forsberg teaches technical and professional writing in the English Department at Western Washington University. She is co-president of the International Jacques Ellul Society and is on the CCSN/Integratio Press editorial board as well as a Faculty Fellow with Faculty Commons.

Lauren E. Futrell Dunaway is a Registered Dietitian and Public Health Researcher with public health teaching, research, and evaluation experience. She teaches graduate and undergraduate courses in the Tulane Celia Scott Weatherhead School of Public Health and Tropical Medicine.

Cantice Greene is professor of English at Clayton State University in Morrow, Georgia. Her professional interests include rhetoric and composition, creative writing, women's studies, applied linguistics, student success, and faith formation in college.

Verónica A. Gutiérrez directs the Great Books Program *en español* for the Angelicum Academy and serves as tutor for Hildegard College, a Great Books institution. Her scholarship and teaching focus on the origins of Mexican Catholicism, challenging myths about native peoples of the Americas.

Bill Hager has been on staff with Cru for 49 years, serving in the faculty ministry (Faculty Commons) for the past 32 years where he is currently the regional director for the Northeast and edits the Missional Moment blog. He lives in Habersham County, Georgia with his wife Jan.

Heather Holleman is an associate teaching professor of advanced writing at Penn State. A speaker and author of several books, she also serves with Faculty Commons, the faculty ministry of Cru.

David Lyle Jeffrey is Distinguished Professor Emeritus of Literature and Humanities at Baylor University. He is a medievalist and a widely published scholar of biblical tradition in western literature and art.

Ruthann Knechel Johansen is Professor Emerita at the University of Notre Dame, President Emerita of Bethany Theological Seminary, and is a poet and author of several books.

Balint Kacsoh teaches integrated basic medical sciences to first-year and second-year MD students at Mercer University School of Medicine. He is the author of *Endocrine Physiology* (a medical school textbook) and the translator of *The Frontier Garrison* by Jenő Rejtő.

Craig T. McMahan is University Minister and Dean of the Chapel at Mercer University. He teaches in the Department of Religion and is the director of Mercer on Mission, a global aid service-learning program that has been responsible for fitting over 23,000 prosthetic legs and hands for amputees in Southeast Asia.

Joseph McRae Mellichamp is Professor Emeritus of Management Science in the Manderson Graduate School of Business at the University of Alabama where he served as a faculty member from 1969 to 1994. He is one of the original founders of Faculty Commons.

Matthew K. Minerd is a Ruthenian Catholic, husband, and father, who serves as a professor of philosophy and moral theology at the Byzantine Catholic Seminary in Pittsburgh, Pennsylvania.

A. Chase Mitchell is Associate Professor of Media and Communication at East Tennessee State University, where he directs the Technical and Professional Writing program. His scholarly work has appeared in venues such as *Christian Scholar's Review*, *FaithTech*, and *Christ and Pop Culture*.

Chinekwu Obidoa is Professor of Global Health Studies at Mercer University, Macon, Georgia, and a life coach who specializes in helping young people discover their calling and vocation.

Eric M. O'Dell was born in the Blue Ridge mountains of Virginia and raised in the panhandle of Florida, Eric graduated from Mercer University. He returned to Macon after earning an MFA in studio art at Florida State University. He and his wife Greta live near Mercer's campus, where Eric teaches art and maintains an active studio practice in downtown Macon.

Jack L. Sammons is the Griffin B. Bell Professor of Law Emeritus at Mercer University School of Law. The author of publications on a variety of subjects and in a variety of genres, he currently lives in Thetford Center, Vermont, and is a member of St. Thomas Episcopal Church at Dartmouth College.

Michael D. Torre has taught philosophy at the University of San Francisco for the past forty years. He was the second General Editor and eighth President of the American Maritain Association. He has written many articles for it and published several books, chiefly on God's permission of sin.

John G. Trapani Jr. is Professor Emeritus of philosophy at Walsh University in North Canton, Ohio, where he taught for 44 years. He is the author of two books and over 35 published essays and book chapters, most of them on philosopher Jacques Maritain.

James W. Vining is an Associate Professor of Communication Studies at Governors State University in suburban Chicago. Jim spent 15 years in pastoral ministry in various contexts before entering academia. His primary research interests relate to the intersections of religion and public rhetoric.

Anna N. Walker is a medical doctor who is board certified in Anatomic and Clinical Pathology. She is Professor Emerita of Pathology at Mercer University School of Medicine in Macon, Georgia.

Daniel Williams is Director of Mercer University's Archives, Special Collections, and Digital Initiatives Department. He has also taught several Integrative Studies classes on campus and serves as a supply preacher in the Middle Georgia area.

Mark A. E. Williams is a former Oxford Research Fellow and a Professor Emeritus in the Communication Studies Department at California State University, Sacramento. His research focuses on Classical rhetoric as well as rhetoric and religion. His most recent book is *Just Words* from Integratio Press.

Ralph C. Wood is University Professor Emeritus of Theology and Literature at Baylor University in Waco, Texas. He is a prominent scholar on the works of Flannery O'Connor, among other writers.

Introduction

Why publish yet another devotional book? There is, after all, an abundance of that genre available to believers these days, some by such excellent writers as Oswald Chambers, Charles Spurgeon, C. S. Lewis, and Dallas Willard. That, I grant, is a legitimate question, and I hope my readers will agree that the following reply is acceptable.

Here's what awaits you as you read this book: Authors in this collection will challenge us to take seriously the command to perform our academic duties as unto the Lord. The contributors and the publisher have agreed to undergird the entire process with prayer. We have endeavored to make available to university faculty all over the English-speaking world the wisdom that has come through many decades of service to the Academy as people of faith in Jesus the Christ. The authors have earned many academic honors as well as performed innumerable selfless missions in an effort to bring a redemptive Christian presence to their colleges and universities.

There is not a single devotional book available, to my knowledge, that is directed exclusively to post-secondary faculty as an audience. Of course, non-Christian readers, whether they are teachers or not, are warmly welcomed too, but Christian professors are our focus. Every single contributor to this volume holds faculty rank at the university level and is a professing Christian. I've asked all of them to include in every single meditation a pertinent scripture quotation and to make a direct connection with the teaching life—whether the classroom, research, participation in campus life and professional organizations, or simply relationships in the academic community. I've also asked them to write with the preeminent goal of always lifting up Jesus of Nazareth as Savior and Lord.

I personally have found thoughtful, spiritually mature, and sensitive meditations immensely helpful in keeping my own personal daily devotionals renewed. It has been widely observed that our communication with God comes more vibrantly alive when it is stoked with godly thoughts that we can glean from great saints of both the present and the past.

In one excellent devotional book I recently found a passage that speaks powerfully about the vital importance of establishing a habit of daily personal worship. The late Dr. Dennis Kinlaw (President of Asbury University in Wilmore, Kentucky) refers to God's directions to Moses for building the tabernacle: "Have them make a sanctuary for me, so that I may dwell among them" (Exod. 25:8, TLV). Then he writes:

> God's position is to be the center of our daily social life—indeed, of our total life. The key element in the true Christian life is a daily experience of worship and adoration of God as the center of our personal existence. . . . . Anything that forces you into the presence of Christ and into an openness to his Word will make a dramatic difference in your Christian life. He positions himself right in the middle of our lives so we can look at him and talk to him every day. He wants to tabernacle in us.[4]

University faculty members in the United States who are followers of Jesus face a prevailing culture that is anything but supportive of their daily walk with the Lord. Their own numbers, as well as those of the students in their classes, are dwindling at a troubling rate, according to recent surveys. They sorely need encouragement from their peers in order to live an upstream teaching and publishing career in the American Academy. They also need practical insights into how to be faithful to their double calling to following Jesus while demonstrating professional and intellectual excellence and integrity.

Over the decades of my academic career, I have been blessed to know personally—or study under—several master teachers who were also Christ-followers: my mentor Wallace Fowlie, poet Dana Gioia, philosophers Dallas Willard and Jean-Louis Chrétien, Michael Edwards, and Mercer's Joseph Hendricks, to name only a few. I've also been inspired in the course of my research by studying the lives and writings of iconic teachers like Jacques Maritain, Simone Weil, and Dietrich Bonhoeffer. In each case, my model teachers have been like Chaucer's Cleric, who "gladly learned" as well as gladly taught.[5] They all had to study and learn extensively long before they attempted to teach. And once they began their teaching careers, they listened to their students and were willing to learn from them. Humility is of crucial importance if a professor aspires to be like the Master Teacher of all time, who learned for three decades before beginning his brief but incomparable teaching tenure.

Graduate programs charged with training prospective college teachers typically have historically addressed only matters of professional competency in teaching and research, but Christian professors today may find resources to inspire and equip them to take seriously their responsibility to live out their calling from God as well as to achieve excellence in teaching and scholarship. Faculty Commons (the faculty ministry of Cru), InterVarsity Fellowship, The Society of Professors in Christian Education, and organizations of

Christian professors in a number of fields in higher education are useful resources.

Finally, a word about our title. "Minding our heart" is a phrase that appears in Proverbs 4:23: "Above all else, guard your heart, for everything you do flows from it" (NIV). In the King James Version, it reads: "Keep thy heart with all diligence; for out of it are the issues of life." My prayer is that the meditations that follow on these pages will help you guard and keep your heart focused on our invisible Advocate, who is the source of the resurrection life that the academic world—our students and our colleagues—so desperately need in our day.

1

Blessings in the Challenge:
Part 1, The Challenge

"You are the salt of the earth. But if the salt loses its saltiness, how can it be made salty again? It is no longer good for anything, except to be thrown out and trampled underfoot. You are the light of the world. A town built on a hill cannot be hidden. Neither do people light a lamp and put it under a bowl. Instead, they put it on its stand, and it gives light to everyone in the house. In the same way, let your light shine before others, that they may see your good deeds and glorify your Father in heaven."

Matthew 5:13–16, NIV

One morning in 1995 during my personal time with God, I strongly felt that he wanted me to be "saltier" and "brighter" as a professor. I was disappointed that I had not done more for Christ as a professor and was wondering whether I was the only Christian faculty member at the University of Georgia. It was quite a pity party! I prayed that God would show me a way to be "brighter" and "saltier."

A few days later a man whom I didn't know, Bill Hager,

stopped by my office. He told me about the University of Georgia's Christian Faculty Forum (CFF). I had no clue such a group existed; however, it was very encouraging. I was definitely not alone at University of Georgia, and I became very involved. A few years later, the CFF participated in sponsoring a Veritas Forum at the University of Georgia. One of the speakers was Walter Bradley, a professor from Texas A and M. Professor Bradley suggested a number of ways professors could have a greater impact for Christ. He emphasized the great opportunities we have to serve him in the University. One of his suggestions was to identify yourself as a follower of Jesus to your students.

The first year I did this, 1999, four or five students came up to me after class. Some thanked me, and several stated that they didn't know that you could be a scientist and a Christian (a common misconception). Later my wife Cheryl and I decided to invite the class to our home for dinner and a discussion on the relationship between science and faith. I handed out a written invitation to my class and about 25 students attended. We had a wonderful time.

We did this again the next year and again had a wonderful dinner and discussion. However, this time a professor in plant biology, the faculty advisor for an atheist group on campus called The Sagan Society, complained to the University Council that I was intimidating students, even though no students in my class had complained to me or to my department chair. The front-page headline in the *Athens Banner Herald* the next day was "Professor: Students intimidated by fliers for colleague's talks." This resulted in several exchanges between myself and the university's president, as well as with my department chair.

Before we began having these dinner discussions, we wondered "What if someone complains?" We prayed and that challenge came, but we both felt very much at peace. The Lord assured us that what we had done was what he wanted us to do. There is nothing like that kind of peace.

"Therefore, since we have been justified through faith, we have peace with God through our Lord Jesus Christ, through whom we have gained access by faith into this grace in which we now stand." (Romans 5:1–2a, NIV)

— **Russ Carlson**, Biochemistry and Molecular Biology, University of Georgia

2

Blessings in the Challenge:
Part 2, The Blessings

"Blessed are you when people insult you, persecute you
and falsely say all kinds of evil against you because of me."

Matthew 5:11, NIV

At the time of this challenge to us, Cheryl and I did not know what the results would be, positive or negative. I suppose, to be honest, I expected bad results. Nevertheless, we had peace from the Lord that we had done the right thing. However unexpectedly for me, the results were not bad. In fact, we received numerous blessings.

One blessing I experienced was the faithfulness of my University of Georgia Christian Faculty Forum (CFF) colleagues. They prayed, they wrote letters to the newspaper, they wrote letters to the president of the university, they encouraged me, and some, who were on important university committees, gave their vocal support.

Secondly, I learned I had colleagues who, even though they may not agree with me, supported me on the basis of academic freedom. Their view was "If you can't discuss this issue (faith and science) in a university, where can it be discussed?" In fact, my department chair wrote the university president stating: "I feel strongly in protecting Professor Carlson's rights to discuss his interest in religion, particularly Christianity and science, with any students who are interested in discussing the issues whether they are religious or not."

Thirdly, this challenge made it possible for me to more freely express my faith in God. Students and colleagues both felt it was okay to discuss issues of faith and science with me. I have been asked to speak on this topic on numerous occasions, and I have done so even though I am probably not the most elegant spokesperson for some of these matters. Many doors were opened! I am very thankful for this freedom.

Over the years since that challenge, I have received many questions and comments from students. An example is an email from a student named Jennifer. In her email she stated, "Your actions have inspired me to stand up for my beliefs and to spread the word of Jesus Christ our Savior and Lord." She apparently sent a copy of her email to her father Ted, and I also received an email from him. Ted was a high school physics teacher with many troubling questions regarding Christianity and science and he wrote, "I am hoping that a Christian viewpoint from a college-level scientist like yourself can clear up some problems that I have not been able to totally resolve over the years." Ted came to Athens and we had a lunch discussion. Six months later, I received an email from Ted's other daughter, Lauren. She wrote: "I just wanted you to know I've been praying for my father's salvation for 11 years. I've specifically been praying that God would put people in his life who know the Lord and have been able to reconcile their scientific beliefs with their faith. I feel like your interest in sharing with him is a direct answer to my prayers."

Romans 5:3b–5 (NIV) says:

We know that suffering produces perseverance; perseverance, character; and character, hope. And hope does not put us to shame, because God's love has been poured out into our hearts through the Holy Spirit, who has been given to us.

The challenge to us resulted in new opportunities and many blessings. I would hardly classify our experience as "suffering", but even if the results had been negative, I know that the Lord would have given us the same hope, peace, and blessings that come simply from doing something he wanted us to do.[6]

— **Russ Carlson**, Biochemistry and Molecular Biology, University of Georgia

3

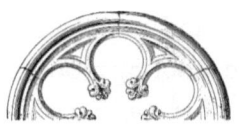

Amid Unfixable Brokenness,
I Saw the Face of God in Vietnam

"Surely he hath borne our griefs and carried our sorrows."

Isaiah 53:4a, KJV

My dad was a "fixer." When the transmission went out on our 1964 Rambler, he fixed it with little more than a screwdriver and a pair of pliers. When the toaster stopped toasting, he took it apart, found the problem and fixed it. When the water pipe broke late on a cold January night, he dug down through the frozen Hoosier soil, discovered the leak and fixed it. He would take on a problem and find a way to fix it. I was his sidekick on these fixing adventures, and so, I grew up believing that the world was "fixable." Things, all kinds of things—cars, toasters, water pipes—would eventually break, but with persistence and elbow grease, they could all be fixed.

That confident childhood naiveté has, over the years, evolved into a more measured view of reality. Some things break that cannot be fixed. Sadly, it is often those things that are most dear to us that are not fixable.

I was reminded of this in Vietnam one recent summer. Our

Mercer on Mission team of faculty and students was fitting amputees with prosthetic legs and hands in the city of Ben Tre. At the end of one very long day, a husband brought his wife to our clinic. He carried her on his back. She had lost most of her right leg in an accident and could not walk. She moved on the floor in an animal-like scooting motion. The woman wore, undisguised, the marks of her age and station. Her face was gaunt and weathered. Her arthritic hands were thin and twisted. Her hair and clothes were unkempt. Toothless and wordless, she made indiscernible grunting sounds in an attempt to communicate. This broken woman had lost so much of what seems to make us human. And yet, here she came to us on the back of her smiling husband.

Several of us left our current patients to see if we could help. We made all the measurements, constructed the appropriate socket and assembled prosthetic components. She was ready to walk. But she could not. Her muscles were too weak. Two of us, one under each arm, lifted her on her new prosthesis. Her husband stood in front, coaxing her forward. But she could not walk. We tried and tried to find a way to help her walk, even to take one step. It was not to be. Eventually, we realized that we could not "fix" this broken woman.

We sent her home with many heartfelt goodbyes. Her husband picked her up and put her on his back like he had done thousands of times before and would do a thousand more. He walked away with a smile, grateful that we had tried to help his wife. I learned later that he carried her like this everywhere he went. Everywhere! This badly broken woman, who gave every appearance of being nothing but a burden, was carried by her husband with an unreasonable gladness that only the purest love could imagine.

I write these words on September 11th, 2023, aware that we live in a very broken world, where sometimes even the most basic humanity seems to be missing, amputated. In such a world, I am convinced that it is our highest calling to do all that we can to fix what has been broken, to repair what has been damaged, to heal what has been wounded.

And yet, on this day, in particular, I am also soberly reminded that not everything can be fixed, not every wound healed. So what do we do with all this unfixable brokenness and unhealable woundedness—in the world, in others and in ourselves? We could become bitter with complaining. We could become hostile in resisting. We could drop our hands and walk away in resignation. But we could also choose another path, the one chosen by this unknown man whom I happened to meet one night half a world away. We could carry the brokenness in love as he did. Without complaining, resisting, or abandoning, we could decide to hold what is unfixable in love.

To hold brokenness in love is not easy. It surely wasn't easy for my Vietnamese friend who carried his wife. Broken things and broken people can be quite heavy. To carry them demands great strength, poured out in humility, patience, courage, and of course, love. The only reward is being a part of the Great Love that still holds the world, and for some, that is enough.

I will never forget my friend's face. For me, it was the face of God.

— **Craig T. McMahan**, University Minister, Dean of Chapel, Assistant Professor of Religion, Mercer University

4

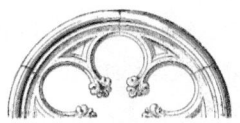

Broken Dreams: Not My Plan

"But before they were born, before they had done anything good or bad, she received a message from God. This message shows that God chooses people according to his own purposes."

Romans 9:11, NLT

"Count it all joy, my brothers, when you meet trials of various kinds for you know that the testing of your faith produces steadfastness."

James 1:2–3, ESV

"He will not suffer thy foot to be moved: he that keepeth thee will not slumber. Behold, he that keepeth Israel shall neither slumber nor sleep."

Psalm 121:3–4, KJV

It is not easy to learn that your future career plans have been halted. Interviewing and applying for a larger leadership role in our university is a good thing. Being passed over is a bitter disappointment, knowing that you were the best candidate and should have been chosen! A great purpose to lead and transform, according to my thinking, has been halted.

Understanding the immediate action is very difficult or even impossible to discern. Why is it so hard for me to accept that my plan, my intentions, my logic is not God's?

Later, the reason for the pause becomes clearer as the days, weeks, and months progress. It was not necessarily a question of wrong planning. But it is a question of whether you can accept the rejection (God saying no) and then patiently wait to discover the new plan. After considerable loss of sleep, I turned to scripture study and reflection, and the situation began to make some sense.

If my plan did not work, then should I feel guilty about not being aligned with God? No! Accepting a new reality combined with an understanding that change and cooperation are going to show a new direction are the beginning steps to getting on the right path. Finally, understanding that it was just my pride and over-confidence that needed attention. The rejection worked to get me on the true path with the right attitudes and motives. My prior focus on a desire to be given the position and honor is now transformed into a future direction to become a servant leader. The hubris is what was being altered.

How often does pride enter into our life? Too often I know. Are we being sensitive to God's direction? Shouldn't we ask for sensitivity to discover the redirection? Can we realize that when God says no, it means he has a better way? Should we not support his plan with humility and cooperation? I think so.

— **William F. Bina**, Medicine, Mercer University

5

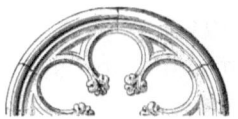

Redeeming the Time

"Thine eyes did see my substance, yet being unperfect; and in thy book all my members were written, which in continuance were fashioned, when as yet there was none of them."

Psalm 139:16, KJV

When I finished my doctorate from a fine institution, with a widely known figure as my mentor, I had expectations of becoming a publishing scholar at a major research university. However, the job market for new positions in the humanities in the early seventies bottomed out, and the only position I was offered was from a small teaching institution. Furthermore, the salary was significantly lower than I had been told I should expect. We were bitterly disappointed.

Twenty years later, after working hard at that small university to improve my credentials and gaining valuable experience in the classroom, I was still unable to land an attractive offer. I felt underpaid, underappreciated, and deeply discouraged.

What turned things around for me and brought me out of my confusion and entrapment? I wish I could say that I had an epiphany and lifted myself out of my discouragement the way David "encouraged himself in the Lord" (1 Sam. 30:6, KJV) after the crushing defeat at Ziklag. Instead, the Lord in his kindness orchestrated a number of key changes in my life.

First, I was invited to get in on the ground level of designing a Great Books Program at our university. The new program not only helped me transition from the lecture method to the seminar method in the classroom. It also gave me access to a broader cross-section of the student body, as did the Senior Capstone Program, an interdisciplinary rubric that enabled me to teach on topics outside my specialization: race relations, compelling moral and ethical issues, even a class on "Stories of Calling in Literature." I now began to feel more a part of the larger university and broadened my collegial relationships as well. My university was doing a better job of recruiting: students were brighter and more diverse, and relationships with my students became an increasingly important part of my teaching life.

In the late 1990s, a couple of colleagues and I started a Faculty/Staff Christian Fellowship on campus, and I got involved in networking with Christian faculty all over the country. All this led me to explore how to frame my teaching and scholarship in the context or matrix of my faith. In 2000, the Mercer Commons, A Center for Faith, Learning, and Vocation, was created with a $2.9 million grant from the Lilly Foundation, and I was appointed a Senior Fellow. For three years my teaching load was reduced in order to provide ample time for research on vocation and calling in the academic enterprise. In 2003 I was appointed Director of the Commons. This, I told myself, was the perfect job for me. I could continue to teach French and Interdisciplinary Studies, pursue my research, and organize programs designed to strengthen the role of Mercer's religious heritage. We organized colloquia, lecture series, and symposia on the relationships of faith and learning, faith and poetry, race relations, and the religious history of our college. We even started an annual week-long summer faculty workshop on faith, learning, and vocation.

My academic work was now much more fully integrated with my faith journey. I have to wonder how much I would've missed if I'd been offered the job at that major research university. I never could have foreseen the itinerary that my own vocation would follow, or what new opportunities were to come my way where I was. Unbeknownst to us, "My Father is always working," as Jesus says in John 5:17 (KJV). And, as the Country music supergroup Rascal Flats once sang, "God blessed the broken road."[7]

— **John Marson Dunaway**, French and Interdisciplinary Studies, Mercer University

6

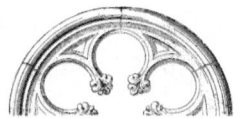

Chosen to Grieve

"Bear one another's burdens, and thereby fulfill the law of Christ."

Galatians 6:2, NASB

Snow crunched beneath my boots as I hurried onto Penn State's campus early one February morning. A first-year student in the Master of Fine Arts program, I was a Graduate Teaching Fellow assigned to English 15, an introductory rhetoric class. Moments after commencing, a student in the back row jumped up, dodging the puddles of melted snow on the tile as she dashed past me out the door. Several times during class she whisked by me. When the period ended, she lingered to apologize, and I suggested that if she felt ill, she should stay home. She gazed at me solemnly and told me, with eyes full of sadness, that she was pregnant.

The student's most recent paper flashed in my mind, a persuasion piece arguing decisively against abortion, for choosing life in all circumstances, using a metaphor of a car ride, the details of which now elude me. Gazing back at her, I realized I was no more than six years older than this student.

"Considering the topic of your last paper," I finally remarked, "you must have given this lots of thought." She shook her head, saying she wrote it before she was pregnant, but that she had always been pro-life. "Oh, so then you'll . . ." I began. She shrugged, indecision in her eyes. Sharing with her that I, too, had always been pro-life, I suggested we meet for coffee. I even gave her my phone number. Sniffling, she nodded and walked away.

Though the student initially confided in me (she had not yet told her parents), she eventually pulled away. I suspected her friends had convinced her not to engage with her pro-life teacher. Unsure what to do, I pulled back too.

For weeks I prayed for her, infusing our in-class interactions with love. For weeks she hid beneath sweatpants and baggy sweatshirts, unkempt hair held back in a headband, a silent presence in the back row. The longer she remained pregnant, the greater grew my hope that she would choose life. Maybe God put me in this class for this reason.

One morning, she marched past me into class, blow-dried hair trailing softly behind her. Mid-conversation with someone, I watched as she turned, wearing jeans and a crop-top exposing her midriff beneath a full-length fur-lined winter coat. She slid into her seat, looking glamorous. I knew, without a word, that she had had an abortion.

I don't remember how I got through class or when I began shaking. Finally alone, tears I could no longer contain spilled out as sobs as I erased the chalkboard. Was this my fault? Should I have tried harder? Was this a test from God that I had failed? Remembering a Pregnancy Resource Center near campus, I made my way there. "You are grieving this baby," a counselor comforted me gently. "Someone needs to grieve this baby, and God chose you, but know that this is not your fault." It was not my fault.

Over twenty years have passed, yet the pain of that moment remains, even as this student frequents my prayers. It's especially poignant because four years ago today, I lost my unborn daughter early in pregnancy, deeply hurt that God would send me a child, only to take her away. Wouldn't it have been better not to send me or the student a child at all? But God formed both these babies, knowing, from all eternity, the limited length of their days, and loving them.

As educators, we are often drawn into our students' lives in deeply personal ways, feeling sorrow at their sorrow, and joy at their joy. We guide them and pray with them, and when they make the wrong choices, we often feel like we've failed. That's because we don't see what God sees.

I'll never know, in this life at least, why God placed me, an inexperienced twenty-something graduate student, in a classroom with a pregnant teenager contemplating abortion. But he did. What I take from this is that we need to trust that God puts us where he needs us. Perhaps we will change hearts. Or perhaps our only role will be to listen and serve as a signpost for Truth.

— **Verónica A. Gutiérrez**, History, Hildegard College

Our Work as Worship

"I appeal to you therefore, brothers, by the mercies of God, to present your bodies as a living sacrifice, holy and acceptable to God, which is your spiritual worship."

Romans 12:1, ESV

C hristian faculty members at secular schools recognize that the spiritual-secular dichotomy is a fiction, a false reality. In God's sight, there is no spiritual versus secular realm—no part of his creation into which he does not reach, no person so lost he cannot save, nothing so corrupted by sin he cannot redeem. Likewise, there is no division between the natural and supernatural realms, for God sustains all of reality. The Dutch Calvinist theologian Abraham Kuyper, who also served a term as Prime Minister of the Netherlands, said: "There is not a square inch in the whole domain of our human existence over which Christ, who is Sovereign over all, does not cry: 'Mine!'"[8]

While we understand that being in fellowship with Christ means that "this world is not my home," Kuyper's words also affirm the glorious truth that "this IS my father's world"—the world that he created in love, though tainted by sin, which he wills to redeem. And the grand mystery is that he chooses to do this through those of us in the Church, who are the members of Christ's body. Whether at religious or secular universities, we are all his agents of redemption in every part of his world.

But what does that mean for Christian academics? Though we may reject the spiritual-secular dichotomy, we should beware of the temptation to identify the more "spiritual" aspects of our work as faculty members with only certain activities, like comforting students in distress, publicly professing our faith, or participating in prayer meetings with our Christian colleagues. At the same time, we must be even more vigilant against thinking that it is only through our success or productivity or effectiveness as measured by the professional criteria of our discipline or our particular department, through which we might claim to bring him glory.

While striving as an untenured professor to publish research, I recall anxiously praying, "Lord, help me. I'm doing this for you." One day, while working on an article and praying that prayer, I heard God say to me, not in a chiding manner, but just as a matter of fact: "I don't need your tenure." And then he said it again. "I don't need your tenure," which silenced my supplication. But then he went on: "I know it's important to you, and that's okay. But I don't want you to do it *for* me; I want you to do it *with* me." And with the change in that preposition, I experienced a paradigm shift, realizing that the essence of faithfulness was not in doing things for God, but in learning to do everything he has given us to do, with him.

If we can incarnate this reality in our lives, then no matter where God places us, no matter what God has us do, we will change his world for him. So, whether mentoring students, lecturing in class, attending department meetings, or engaging with scholarly criticism at conferences—any activity can be done in faithfulness to God, bringing glory to him and transformation and redemption to the world that he created and dearly loves.

The wonderful, awesome, and mysterious truth about God is that he calls each of us to play a part in his glorious plan, not merely as a dispensable tool, but as his co-workers, his co-laborers. For when we collaborate with God, the mundane becomes imbued with eternal significance: raising a family, working on research, casually talking with colleagues in the hallway—whatever we do, everything we do, when done with God, is transformed into worship. In this way, our lives can become a daily liturgy, a spiritual act of worship, not only benefitting those around us, but bringing glory to our God, who glories in seeking our highest good.

— **Paul Chen**, Political Science,
Western Washington University

8

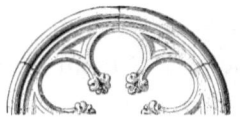

Standing Firm in Truth

"Stand firm then, with the belt of truth buckled around your waist."

Ephesians 6:14a, NIV

As a professor, I have often found myself in situations where speaking the truth was not the easiest option. As an academic advisor, I had to warn a student that his academic performance put him on a trajectory jeopardizing his national board exam; it was not an easy path. However, Ephesians 6:14 reminds us of the importance of standing firm in the truth, even when it is difficult.

This student was offended by my well-intended warning. He had about six months to correct his ways, but his ego was hurt by even the mere suggestion that he could fail the all-important board exam, which had a huge bearing on his residency-matching success at the end of medical school. From that point on, he shunned meeting with me. I learned about his feelings when he came to see me with the news that he had just received the results of his exam, and he had failed. He had the courage to tell me how he had felt about me and my warning and admitted that he was "pig-headed" and wrong. He was desperate and asked for advice on how to overcome his deficit. He probably felt that I would not have ill feelings about him, and I certainly established my credibility with him with the accuracy of my forecast.

The image of the belt of truth in Ephesians 6:14 is a powerful metaphor for the role of truth in our lives. Just as a belt holds everything together and provides support and stability, so, too, does the truth provide a solid foundation for our lives. Without truth, everything else falls apart. This is antithetical to the postmodernist concept of truth. In the postmodernist view, the truth is always contingent on historical and social context rather than being absolute and universal, and that truth is always partial. To postmodernists, the only accepted absolute truth is that there is no absolute truth.

Jesus said, "And you will know the truth, and the truth will set you free" (John 8:32, NLT). My encounter with this student also reminded me of Matthew 7:13–14 (NIV): "Enter through the narrow gate. For wide is the gate and broad is the road that leads to destruction, and many enter through it. But small is the gate and narrow the road that leads to life, and only a few find it." My encounter with this student had a happy ending. He listened, acted on the advice, and succeeded. What won him over was not just truthfulness but that it was offered with *agape*, even if he recognized it belatedly. After so many years, we are still in contact.

In academia, there is supposed to be a constant push and pull between different ideas. From my perspective, this is in the pursuit of the truth. However, in recent years, the debate has been significantly silenced on certain topics, even in medical sciences. Ideological conformity and self-censoring became an expectation and often a must for one's job security and good rapport with the new generation of indoctrinated students. It appeared that postmodernists had found their absolute (and mandatory) truths beyond the aforementioned concept.

After all, the postmodernist view of truth has a sliver of unintended relevance for Christians. As the Apostle Paul wrote in 1 Corinthians 13:9–13 (NIV):

> For we know in part and we prophesy in part, but when completeness comes, what is in part disappears. When I was a child, I talked like a child, I thought like a child, I reasoned like a child. When I became a man, I put the ways of childhood behind me. For now, we see only a reflection as in a mirror; then we shall see face to face. Now I know in part; then I shall know fully, even as I am fully known. And now these three remain: faith, hope, and love. But the greatest of these is love.

Indeed, our understanding is incomplete, even when we earnestly seek the truth. In academia, we must never give up seeking the truth and debating ideas openly, but always with love and caring.

If this is the narrow gate, that is a sure sign that we are on the right path.

— **Balint Kacsoh**, Medicine, Mercer University

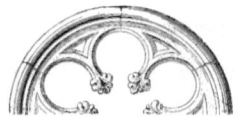

9

A Peddler of Hope

"And we know that in all things God works for the good of those who love him, who have been called according to his purpose."

Romans 8:28, NIV

The start of a new school year always awakens a quiet stirring within my soul, a sense of God's hand at work. It is a feeling that resonates far beyond the crisp scent of a new notebook and the promise of a blank page. It is the palpable sense of possibility that hangs in the August air on a college campus. Like the turning of the leaves, students arrive, each with their own unique story unfolding. There is a beautiful mystery in the connections waiting to be made, the lives about to intersect.

When I first arrived at Mercer University in the fall of 1998, I was struck by something President Kirby Godsey said at a faculty meeting. He reminded us that a "professor is a peddler of hope." That resonated deeply. It is a sentiment echoed in his quote near the fountain in nearby Tattnall Square Park: "We are here to give people hope, to bear light amidst the shadows, to teach, to live out grace." These words are not just about academics; they are about a calling, a ministry.

The very words "college" and "university" speak to this higher purpose. "College" comes from the Latin *collegium*, meaning "partnership," and "university" from *universium*, meaning "everything." And a "professor," at the root of the word, is one who "professes a faith"—a faith in knowledge, in learning, and ultimately, in the potential of each student. It is a sacred trust, a true partnership in growth. This ideal is perhaps best captured by Chaucer's description of the clerk: "And gladly shall he learn and teach."[9]

So how do we make the most of our precious time with students? I often share with them the advice I once read in *The New York Times*: "Widen the circle of human beings who know you and care about you."[10] It echoes the wisdom of Fred Rogers: "Always look for the helpers."[11] I also remind students about cultivating genuine connections, learning to truly listen, asking meaningful questions, and seeking the joy that God places within each of us. As Parker Palmer suggests, "I must listen to my life and try to understand what it is truly about," allowing God to guide our path.[12]

In my First-Year Experience course, I enjoy demonstrating a simple illustration: "The Jar of Life." A translucent mason jar filled first with golf balls (faith, family, friends, freedoms, and health) seems full, yet pebbles (job, house, car) fit in around them. Even sand (the small stresses of life) finds its place. And finally, there is room for two cups of coffee—a reminder to cherish those moments of fellowship, those deep connections that nourish the soul. It is also a reminder to prioritize what truly matters, to center our lives on Christ and his love.

Teaching is more than a job for me; it is a vocation, a calling from God. It is the only path I have ever envisioned. Growing up in North Carolina, watching my parents teach, I knew this was my purpose. I treat each day as a chance to discover something new, to draw closer to God through understanding his creation. This is why I love being a professor, mentoring students, and witnessing their intellectual and personal growth. At its heart, true teaching is about nurturing relationships, fostering those cherished conversations beyond the classroom where students can freely share their beliefs and perspectives.

As graduation nears, seniors will often seek guidance on what they *ought* to do next. Their faith becomes a key source of direction. Many want to connect their spiritual beliefs with their dreams, hoping to use their talents to serve God. It is a privilege to help them discern their calling and step into God's plan for their lives. Our true success as educators is not measured at graduation, but later, by how our students have used their hands and voices to make a difference in the lives of others.

— **Andy D. Digh**, Computer Science, Mercer University

10

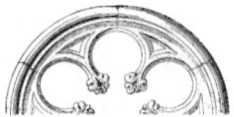

Dialogues with Denise

"For those who exalt themselves will be humbled, and those who humble themselves will be exalted."

Luke 14:11, NLT

I began my teaching career as a very green assistant professor of French, fresh out of graduate school and painfully aware of how many of the great books of the Western world I had yet to read.

One of the best gifts in God's providential care for me during my teaching career was that my closest colleague for the first two decades of my tenure was a Frenchwoman named Denise Juilliard whose literary and spiritual interests were strikingly similar to my own. During the job interview I learned that she had met Julien Green. Green was born in Paris to American parents whose deeply Southern roots imbued his French writings, including his masterpiece *Moïra*, with a yearning for place.

Green was the novelist who was also the subject of my dissertation. My colleague Denise, I learned, had actually met Green in such a remarkable way that he had described the chance encounter on a Paris street in his published *Journal*. Eventually,

Denise married the French novelist Vladimir Volkoff, and I had the privilege of becoming one of his many American friends, and eventually his translator.

Denise and I enjoyed many animated conversations in French. It provided a welcome opportunity to enrich my vocabulary and fluency, but it was also a chance to be mentored by a wise colleague who had an unusually rich knowledge of literature, music, and the arts.

Denise was an exceedingly well-read and cultured French person, but she was comfortable enough in her skin to surprise me at times with a total lack of pretension. I was both shocked and delighted, for instance, when she ordered grits for lunch! Despite her refined culinary tastes, she enjoyed declaring her love for grits, which she considered an exotic treat for a Parisian.

During these fascinating dialogues with Denise, she would often mention a book she had enjoyed and ask me if I'd read it. My frequently embarrassed negative response was never greeted by a supercilious or sarcastic attitude on her part. Instead, she always said something like: "Oh, well, I envy your having that great pleasure to look forward to." Such an admirably gracious remark had the effect of inspiring and encouraging me rather than making me feel defeated, and it was one of the most endearing qualities of this wonderful colleague and friend.

In the academic world, it's a constant temptation to allow our knowledge to make us want to lord it over those who are less well-read than we are. Saint Paul, who was one of the best-educated men of his time, however, wrote in 1 Corinthians 8:1 (NKJV) that "knowledge puffs up, but charity edifies."

Though Denise spoke several languages and had read many more of the great books than I, she had the kindness and humility to be an encourager for me during the formative years of my teaching career. I'll always be grateful to her for that generosity of spirit. While I learned a wealth of French language and culture from her, I also learned from her example that a good mentor must be a gracious encourager.

What quality have you found most helpful in your mentors?

— **John Marson Dunaway**, French and
  Interdisciplinary Studies, Mercer University

11

A Physician Professor Who
Could Not Heal Himself

"All things are of God, who hath reconciled us to himself
by Jesus Christ, and hath given to us the ministry of
reconciliation."

2 Corinthians 5:18, KJV

As a doctoral student at the University of Chicago Divinity School in the latter half of the 1960s, I engorged myself on Protestant liberalism—hook, line, sinker, and pole. In a three-course seminar in the theology of Paul Tillich, I learned that modern secular culture poses questions to which theologians provide answers. Tillich called it the "method of correlation." It is far from a contemptible enterprise. Yet one can hardly stake one's very existence on the proposition that "culture is the shape of religion and religion is the substance of culture."[13] Little, alas, did I heed the warning of Jean Kellogg, an older grad student: "You should remember that the purpose of education in Swift Hall is to turn the wine back into water."

Heedlessly, I took my Chicago sophistication with me to

my first teaching post, at Wake Forest University in 1971. My prim Tillichianism led me to think that my prime mission was to wipe the grins off fundamentalist faces, to rub pious Baptist noses in the cold snows of modern secularity, so that my students would become little liberals like me. During my very first semester, therefore, I taught the modern masters of suspicion—Hemingway and Faulkner, Kafka and Lawrence, Sartre and Camus. Yet I faced a terrible problem. There was not a single fundamentalist to be found! Instead, my classrooms were filled with bright young products of the late 60s, many of them having protested the Vietnam War and experimented with drugs. This often meant that they were either poorly catechized Catholics coming down from the North, or else regional Protestants knowing little about their own tradition.

I was at wit's end. I had been educated for a job that I was grossly unprepared to perform. How could I deepen and revitalize the faith—not only of my students, but chiefly of myself? I was saved from total calamity when I was confronted by the pastor of the campus Baptist church, Warren Carr. He was smarter, tougher, funnier, and more theologically astute than the professors. He had put his life on the line during the civil rights crisis of the 1960s. A Molotov cocktail was thrown onto the roof of his home, and his church was defaced in Durham, North Carolina. Yet Carr always made clear that his courageous stance on race derived from his prior and final commitment to Christ and his church. There alone, he preached, "can we be reconciled to each other because God has first reconciled himself to us?"

Carr had learned this lesson, not from Tillich or Niebuhr, but from Karl Barth. Nothing less than God's total reconciliation of the world to himself in Christ, Carr learned from Barth, can redeem and transform both the finest moral causes as well as the worst moral evils. Far from being a merely private or individual matter, the Barthian Carr insisted, our alienation from God is overcome only in the worship and practices of the community called the Body of Christ. At first, I balked from tackling even a modest portion of the forbidding 10,000 pages of Barth's masterwork with its uninviting title: *Church Dogmatics*. There was still a lingering Tillichianism at work in my conviction that the great monuments of Western art and culture were a sufficient legacy to sustain Christian faith.

A year spent in Italy, 1976–77, cured me of this delusion. The European churches were on their way to becoming mausoleums, even as their civil impact was also dwindling. And so I plunged into the work of Søren Kierkegaard, seeking to find a radical alternative to the collapse of Christendom that he had so acutely diagnosed in the nineteenth century. Eventually I discovered what Kierkegaard himself confessed—that he was a corrective rather than a cure, a way station and not a terminus. Via a long and arduous self-tutelage, I immersed myself in the curative called Karl Barth.

I also began setting Barthian theology in relation to a clutch of writers who helped re-baptize my own imagination as well as to reinvigorate the dormant if not dead Christianity of my students: T. S. Eliot and W. H. Auden, J. R. R. Tolkien and C. S. Lewis, Graham Greene and Walker Percy, Charles Williams and Dorothy L. Sayers. Best of all, I returned to Flannery O'Connor. She arrested the attention of my Wake Forest students like no one else. For the remainder of my fifty years in the collegiate classroom, therefore, I devoted myself to teaching these Protestant and Catholic figures to my Protestant and Catholic students—namely, as a physician-professor who could not heal himself.

— **Ralph C. Wood**, Theology and Literature,
  Baylor University

12

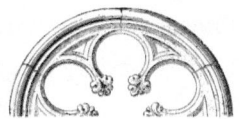

They Shared My Burden

"It is the Lord who goes before you; He will be with you. He will not fail you or abandon you. Do not fear or be dismayed."

Deuteronomy 31:8–9, AMP

When my mother nearly died in January 2022, my students, to my surprise, became my consolation. Two years into the pandemic I had, like many professors who taught during COVID-19, devoted hours to comforting students overwhelmed or depressed by lockdown, afraid of the present and anxious about the future, all while homeschooling my two older children. I was spent.

Days before Spring semester, a COVID-19 outbreak temporarily closed my son's preschool, so I began classes on Zoom with a 4-, 6-, and 8-year-old in the background. Alarmed by my mother's call telling me she had fainted and injured her head, I decided to fly to Phoenix to care for her. Worried that she might have COVID-19, I told students we would meet on Zoom indefinitely. Unsure how to handle my distress, they stared at me blankly through the screen.

COVID-19-induced bilateral pneumonia hospitalized my mother. During those terrifying days, my students, whom I saw on Zoom three days a week, provided unexpected solace, asking for updates, offering prayers, and emailing scriptural encouragement. When Timothy, a graduating history major in a World History Survey populated by freshmen, didn't log off as class ended, I initially found this annoying. I said little, hoping he would stop. But he didn't. He asked how I was, offering me silent space for self-reflection. I found myself grateful for this student's concern.

On days my father lingered at the hospital and I was late getting back to my parents' home to launch class, Timothy started discussion for me. As the weeks passed, I came to see that God had a hand on the situation. It was no accident that Timothy had not taken World History his freshman year; it was providential. God was upholding me via my students.

Living for 75 minutes every four days I was allowed to visit my hospitalized mother, I sustained myself in the meantime by preparing and recording lectures for my flipped classroom, and by discussing primary texts with students over many Zoom sessions; my classes were moments of grace. My teaching schedule meant that I was in more frequent contact with my students than with my family in Los Angeles, able to express to them what I was too exhausted to say to my husband in our whispered late-night phone conversations. Those days are hazy, but the sensation of my students carrying my burden for me is clear.

One Monday night I arrived on the COVID-19 ward only to have a nurse pull me aside, saying the next 24 hours would be critical. When I logged into my Latin American history class on Tuesday afternoon and told my students that I had held my mother's hand the night before and said goodbye, just in case, they wept with me. Before I could transition into class discussion, a student named Elizabeth timidly asked if she could pray for me. As I nodded my consent, she led the class in beautiful words that brought me strength and comfort. On Friday, when it was my turn to see my mother again, Elizabeth emailed to ask if she had made it. She had.

As educators, we may feel called to remain strong for our students, to model a Christian acceptance of adversity or a supernatural joy in hardship. This experience taught me that in moments when we are weak and broken, the Lord may reveal himself to us through our students. The thought of losing my mother without my husband by my side had left me feeling empty and so alone, but the Lord did not forsake me. He spoke to me through not just one, but dozens of voices. My students' voices.

— **Verónica A. Gutiérrez**, History, Hildegard College

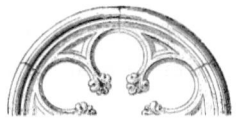

13

The Peace of God,
The Joy of Teaching

"Give all your worries and cares to God, for he cares about you."

1 Peter 5:7, NLT

"Do not be anxious about anything, but in every situation, by prayer and petition, with thanksgiving, present your requests to God. And the peace of God which transcends all understanding will guard your hearts and minds in Christ Jesus."

Philippians 4:6–7, NIV

We're teaching in tough times. In our state, many of the schools in our university system are still reeling from the decreases in the budget that accompanied drops in enrollment during the height of the COVID-19 pandemic. My university, a Predominantly Black Institution, was hit especially hard, suffering a 17% decline in enrollment. As you can imagine, such a steep decline in student numbers (and subsequently enrollment dollars) significantly impacted our campus. Add to that the "Great Resignation," our senior ranking colleagues here and across the country resigning in large numbers, and it's easy to understand the critical situation in which we work every day.

I'd describe the atmosphere within my campus as increasingly nervous. Professors are wondering whether their jobs are in jeopardy. Department chairs wonder if they will be able to offer the supporting services they've come to rely on—the writing centers, tutoring services, and visiting scholar initiatives. Students had already been suffering from increased levels of anxiety, as many of our colleagues' research in mental health has underscored. In the past year, I've had a student ask me twice whether our school is in danger of closing or consolidating with another university.

With the changing atmosphere, I have needed to meditate on the Lord in more concentrated ways to resist the temptation of giving in to anxiety. Two scriptures repeatedly coming to mind are: "Give all your worries and cares to God, for he cares about you" (1 Pet. 5:7, NLT), and "Do not be anxious about anything, but in every situation, by prayer and petition, with thanksgiving, present your requests to God. And the peace of God which transcends all understanding will guard your hearts and minds in Christ Jesus" (Phil. 4:6–7, NIV).

The resulting peace has enabled me to find joy in my everyday tasks, especially in working with students. I was invited to team-teach in an honors Humanities seminar last spring. The smaller class size led to deeper interaction with students. In my portion of the course, I was able to present some of the eighteenth-century writings of Black people, exposing rich narratives of spiritual engagement (especially in the works of Jupiter Hammon and James Ukawsaw Gronniosaw). We also discussed the emergence of the Black church in Savannah,

Georgia. Students' written responses to discussion questions in that class confirmed that they felt edified discussing these early Black writers' personal declarations to and about God as they endured harsh conditions as servants and slaves during the antebellum period of American history. I felt invigorated sharing those narratives that many of the students probably wouldn't have encountered otherwise, since many were pursuing science degrees and other majors outside of English.

The team-teaching opportunity was a reminder that God cares for me. Whatever condition I'm in, he's with me. His presence has brought me peace.

— **Cantice Greene**, English, Clayton State University

14

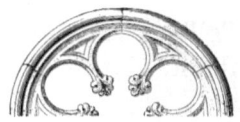

Why Me, Lord?

"Therefore, brethren, be all the more diligent to make certain about His calling and choosing you; for as long as you practice these things, you will never stumble."

2 Peter 1:10, NASB

As a pathologist on a medical school faculty, certainly none of the mission trips in which I participated was all about me. Still, anyone who is going to go on such a trip wants to be useful. I often questioned my purpose since I was not a primary care clinician. Once when I was expressing my doubts, a friend told me that he believed if there was just one person who was helped because a team member was present on the trip, then there was a good reason for that team member to come along. Maybe the following example is the reason I was there.

A woman came to the clinic complaining of a four-week history of fever and abdominal pain. She also brought a lab report with her. She had been seen the week before by a different team and they had sent her to get a particular test. Now, I was not the smartest person in the room, but I was the oldest. Back when I was in high school, we were encouraged to study French, as it was considered the primary international language. I still remember a little bit. All my teammates had studied Spanish.

My medical training stretches back to a time when we sometimes did a medical laboratory test on a patient's blood to detect antibodies against *Salmonella typhi*, the cause of typhoid fever. It was called the Widal test, after the physician who developed it in the early 1900s. None of my younger colleagues had even heard of it, as this test has been replaced by other diagnostic methodologies in the United States. In any case, this patient had a laboratory form with results in French stating that her Widal test was strongly positive. That result along with her clinical findings suggested that she indeed had typhoid, which is not uncommon in that part of the world, where there is no clean water and no sanitation system. I was able to say with some confidence to our team that this patient's treatment should include antibiotics that would be effective against typhoid. I was able to do so not because I knew more infectious disease medicine than the others, but because of my age and experience. Maybe that is why I had been called to be on the mission team.

Each one of us is a unique combination of abilities, knowledge, and experiences. I do believe that God can and will make use of every one of us as he sees fit. One doesn't have to go to Haiti or some other far-off place to serve. We should not be afraid to offer our own combination of gifts and should not feel like these gifts are any less useful or valuable than those of other people whom we might consider smarter or more talented. And I would also remind all of us, myself most of all, to be grateful and to find joy in each day.

— **Anna N. Walker**, Medicine, Mercer University

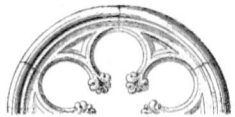

15

See How the Holy Spirit Works!

"I press toward the mark for the prize of the high calling
of God in Christ Jesus."

Philippians 3:14, KJV

What moves a person to choose to become a college professor? Since doing so is not likely a fulfillment of some
childhood dream, there generally is a series of events that lead
future educators to make a mature decision that, while changing their lives, also commits them to a profession that assists
others in changing theirs. But are these events a wholly natural series of chance occurrences, or are they under the gentle
guidance of the Holy Spirit? The perennial problem is clear: are
a person's life-altering events the result of good luck or divine
providence? Answering this question personally can be spiritually tricky business; however, since God plays the long game,
retrospectively, one may sometimes have real confidence about
the occurrence of divine intervention—at least I know that I do.

As a person of faith looking back on my own journey, I now
see that it has been divinely guided all along. Upon completion
of my undergraduate degree in philosophy, I planned to pursue

graduate study in music. Amusingly, God, in his infinite wisdom, had other ideas. 1968 was the peak of the draft call for the Vietnam war and, since I had moral misgivings about my participation in this war, my counter-intuitive solution was to enlist; doing so meant an additional year of service, a guaranteed one-year state-side assignment, and I would be a trumpet player. To me, this threefold combination was a combat-avoiding gamble worth the risk.

Six months after basic training, sure enough, I received orders for Vietnam; fortunately, my one-year state-side guarantee saved me. Then, two months after that, the Army shipped me off to Germany where I did have a providential, life-altering encounter when I overheard a Vietnam combat veteran enthuse about how much he loved "killing gooks!" Horrified, my thinking turned to the significant role that truth plays in human life, and as this thinking consumed me, I practiced less and read more, with St. Thomas Aquinas and his twentieth-century French Catholic disciple, Jacques Maritain, topping the list.

After military service, this providential redirection led me to graduate school in Thomist philosophy where, with course work completed, again, the Holy Spirit interceded when Catholic Walsh College (now University) hired me. Pedagogically motivated by my commitment to a Christian, values-based education, I used some philosophically serious rational thinking to enhance and undergird my students' faith in God. Specifically, several courses enabled me to explain to my students that, since all created beings are contingent, they require the metaphysically prior existence of a non-contingent or necessary being who brings them into existence. St. Thomas called this philosophical Supreme Being the *Ipsum Esse Subsistens* (the Self-subsisting Act-of-Existing), and he rightly identified this

Creator-God as the One who revealed his name to Moses: "I am who am" (Exod. 3:14, Douay-Rheims Bible). Since many students found the philosophical details of this fundamental metaphysical insight speculatively difficult, I was very happy to find a snippet from a poem by Elizabeth Barrett Browning that captured this same idea poetically:

Earth's crammed with Heaven
And every common bush afire with God;
But only he who sees takes off his shoes—
The rest sit 'round it and pluck blackberries.[14]

Indeed, this "earth-crammed-with-Heaven" is nothing less than a manifestation of the goodness, beauty, and holiness of God's creation, scripturally expressed through God's voiceless silence: "Be still, and know that I am God" (Ps. 46:10a, NIV). Remarkably, Browning links this reverential awareness with the essential human need to kneel in the presence of the Holy.

After 44 years in the classroom, I do not know whether I led any of my students to a deep interior friendship with God, despite my desire to do so. What I do know is that, using me, the Holy Spirit sows spiritual seeds, blows them where it will (John 3:8), and guides all of us on our personal journeys. And after that, it's time to "let go and let God" as the motto of Walsh University says: "*sed Deus dat incrementum*" (1 Cor. 3:6–7).[15] That is, although our spiritual work is only as successful as God's will allows, in the end, it is always God, working through us and the Holy Spirit, who gives the increase.

— **John G. Trapani Jr.**, Philosophy, Walsh University

16

Living Heritage

"Therefore, this is what the Sovereign LORD says: 'Look!
I am placing a foundation stone in Jerusalem, a firm and
tested stone. It is a precious cornerstone that is safe to
build on. Whoever believes need never be shaken.'"

Isaiah 28:16, NLT

Joe Hendricks was a legend. In many ways Hendricks, who
spent several decades at the university as student, campus
minister, administrator, and professor was the moral compass
of Mercer, taking the lead in the voluntary desegregation of
the institution in 1963. At the opening of a new academic year
recently, the faculty read an interview with the late Professor
Hendricks that started a free-wheeling discussion about "Our
Mercer Heritage."

The interview with Joe was new to me but was vintage material. It was reassuring to have these remarks from Joe, and it was
nice not to be discussing assessment, administrative initiatives
or what to include on our syllabus verbiage.

When discussion began, it was conversational vertigo for
me. People were quoting Joe Hendricks, there was back and

forth about what people meant to say, what would they say to-day, how far we have come. I was in a room where the majority of my colleagues had never met Joe. Desegregation, Heritage, Justice, Legacy, Diversity, Curriculum, Privilege. People making points and asking for clarification and making conjecture about the past and diagnosing the present state of academics in these terms. And I was dizzy, addled, everyone poking around the words and works of a former professor and profoundly real person I had known and highly respected.

Part of my unease was realizing it would be convenient to frame folks you've known like a painting, a big baroque gold-leafed frame placed firmly and tightly around the edges of a memory to emphasize its importance yet also put a shiny border around who they were and what they did. This was important to talk about, these things Joe had said, and it was good that the institution was orienting itself toward these words. Once recognizing a heritage, how does one proceed?

In late summer, 1997, I needed a loan to wrap up renovation of a home we were buying.

At the bank, sitting behind the desk was a lady named Pearlie Toliver. In the course of our conversation, we realized that both of us were Mercerians. We discovered the intersection of Joe Hendricks that we shared. In that moment, her appearance in our lives was a mercy and a grace that I cannot explain.

Wednesday, February 1st, 2023. Founders' Day. I'm in my office putting on my robe. Through my window over the front door of Hardman I see capped and gowned faculty assembling on the sidewalk. The organ starts up and we begin to process. I find myself seated directly in sight of the podium.

And there she is, our featured speaker. Pearlie Toliver. For a moment I'm 27, getting a mortgage. I was in a place of deep familiarity, in the presence of a lady who had known the folks my current colleagues would read about, and she had let me buy a house in a desperate time. Mercy and grace.

I learned how real and hard her journey to and through Mercer was. How difficult the hard realities of desegregation felt for the first wave of those who had to live it. She had become part of a moment so very important, and she would not gloss over the fact that it was very, very difficult.

Beyond the regalia and the gilded frames, and despite the stagnation of workshops and committees, there is the flesh-and-blood of *faith* and *mercy* and *grace* and *suffering* and *mystery* and *eyes* that *see* and *ears* that *hear*. A country boy from Talbot County and a girl of color from the other side of Tattnall Square Park: maybe these are the corners of the frames of Heritage.

Sometimes I find myself in the University Center with students and I'll point to the painting of Joe and try to explain. I've heard the story of Joe standing up in a meeting when a speaker asked, "What do you believe?" and he said, I think, "Jesus Christ died for me." Imagine today if someone stood up and said the same.

— **Eric M. O'Dell**, Art, Mercer University

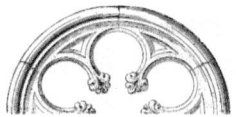

17

Underserved Students?

"When you did it to one of the least of these my brothers and sisters, you were doing it to me."

Matthew 25:40b, NIV

I recall a recent meeting with the former director of the program where I earned my doctorate. After discussing pleasantries, the subject of my online teaching came up. Like many academics who have been reared in the "brick and mortar" world of higher education, he voiced concerns that I myself have felt. What about the learning community? What about mentorship? What about academic rigor? His concerns were not unfounded.

Nonetheless, the conversation got me thinking about why I've never really had many reservations about teaching online. I've actually never taught traditional students. My first teaching assignment was in a very practical evening program at a Catholic college's branch campus. These were all non-traditional students with a certain number of years of work experience before applying to the program. There were also a number of ex-military students. Although I started graduate school a little later than my cohort, I myself was only 30 years old at the time. Imagine trying to teach philosophy—as a core class, in a business program, and to a group of people generally with much more life experience than yourself!

I then started teaching for a small seminary for a small church (the Ruthenian Catholic Church). Since we ordain married men, we get a wide variety of students: sometimes in their 20s. Often, however, older and with significant experience of life and ministry. In our summertime deacon program, we form men who come from many walks of life who sacrifice two weeks to be in Pittsburgh for the experience. Moreover, both at our seminary and at a Roman Catholic seminary, I instruct online students of varying backgrounds, ages, and aspirations.

All the above provides the matrix for an experience that I've repeatedly had from those first days when I taught in Frederick, Maryland. I'm sure you have experienced the following scenario as well. What a blessing when a student comes and thanks you for opening their eyes to a subject previously unknown to them. But what has always been very striking to me is the gratitude that I have received from this "nontraditional" demographic of students in particular. I remember some night school students gratefully remarking: "I had no idea even what philosophy was!" In our yearly deacon program at the seminary, students often comment: "We are grateful that we have time with seminary faculty to receive this kind of teaching in theology for ministry. We would never be able to do this on our own."

But the most striking comments are those I receive as an online instructor, whether personally or through course evaluations. Sometimes, students in their 50s or 60s comment that they never thought they could get a theological or philosophical education, due to the demands of life. At other times, students explain with gratitude how either their own spiritual life or their ministry has been edified by our coursework, sometimes in unexpected ways. Such comments touch my heart, because I grew up in a very poor county in southwestern Pennsylvania. I had dedicated teachers and pastors, but I was not the recipient of the finest education, culture, or preaching. I feel immensely blessed by the wider world that God has opened to a kid who grew up in northern Appalachia.

Online education, despite its weaknesses and difficulties, is a powerful way to share gifts of wonder and knowledge with students who might otherwise be underserved by traditional academic programs. They are, in fact, children of the same Father. Teaching is a "spiritual work of mercy," as the Catholic tradition says. I'm particularly grateful for technology that reaches many who might be passed over by the rigid timeline and requirements of "traditional" instruction.

When our Lord speaks of caring for "the least of [his] brethren" (e.g., Matt. 25:32–46), I believe he includes the "non-traditional" student, who also deserves the bread of truth. When I get frustrated with grading, student questions, or administrative emails, I remind myself what a wonderful gift of Providence it is to have some small ministry in the service of the truth, on behalf of those whom "traditional" academia may not serve.

— **Matthew Minerd**, Philosophy and Moral Theology, Byzantine Catholic Seminary

18

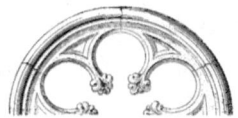

A Pearl of Great Price

"Jesus saith unto him, I am the way, the truth, and the
life: no man cometh unto the Father, but by me."

John 14:6, KJV

That academic work uncovers a pearl of great price, worthy of all our other possessions, has been in full evidence in my lifelong interactions with students. Scholarly responsibilities, as well as decisions in my personal life, have been greatly enriched by my building a close relationship with the religious philosophy of the French thinker and mystic Simone Weil. Her concept of attention, to which I was immediately attracted, added a sacred dimension to my desire to share the joy of learning with others. This extraordinary messenger of God's love elaborates on the part played by desire and joy in studies, which makes of them a preparation par excellence for living a spiritual life. She reminds us that each time we learn a fragment of truth, we approach the pure image of the unique, eternal, and living truth, the very truth, that once in a human voice declared: "I am the way and the *truth* and the life" (John 14:6, NIV, emphasis added).

My serendipitous introduction to Simone Weil's thought took place in the midst of my graduate studies in French language, literature, and culture. As yet unaware of her influence on me but desirous to share the power of this twentieth-century extraordinary mind, I gave an invited presentation to my fellow graduate students. One of my more attentive professors remarked on my close affinity with this unusual thinker and unexpectedly offered to direct my PhD thesis if I chose to write on her. His close attention to the wonder and fulfilment of my own inner needs and aptitudes, discerned in the way I spoke of her, led to a new and infinitely rewarding direction in my life. I, in turn, strive to offer this gift to my students by paying close attention to their intellectual propensities, often just barely beginning to surface.

For Simone Weil, all full attention we give to our work, to our students, to those we love, and to the beauty around us intensifies the devotion we give to prayer. She insists that "Never in any case whatever is a genuine effort of attention wasted."[16] This thought can be a bulwark of support for students, struggling sometimes in despair of grasping some elusive material, if they can maintain their faith that their efforts will invariably bear fruit in unexpected ways.

Weil describes how pure attention requires a suspension of thought, leaving the mind detached, empty, and ready to be penetrated by the object of attention. Learners must hold in their minds the diverse knowledge already acquired and patiently wait for an understanding of the truth to penetrate their thoughts. But they must have their oil lamps well filled as they await the Bridegroom with confidence and desire. It is our job to support their efforts toward being prepared, even when they don't entirely see the end goal.

The message of giving full attention is greatly needed in the contemporary setting of constant distractions with little content, all clamoring for our attention. Educators have no easy task in getting their students to sit calmly and focus their minds on a task at hand; nevertheless, the effort is perhaps more essential than ever. Honing the ability to give attention to those around us who are suffering, as are many of the souls for whom we have responsibility, means having one's own soul ready and waiting to receive the afflicted. This capacity for attention transforms into true love of neighbor, which, as Christ reminds us, is the second and greatest commandment. As educators striving to prepare young minds to imagine a better society, we are well placed to reveal to our students this pearl of great price, worthy of selling our possessions, keeping nothing for ourselves, in order to acquire such a precious gift.

— **E. Jane Doering**, French Literature and Culture, University of Notre Dame

19

James's Cautions for Teachers

"Dear brothers and sisters, not many of you should
become teachers in the church, for we who teach will be
judged more strictly. Indeed, we all make many mistakes.
For if we could control our tongues, we would be perfect
and could also control ourselves in every other way. We
can make a large horse go wherever we want by means of
a small bit in its mouth. And a small rudder makes a huge
ship turn wherever the pilot chooses to go, even though
the winds are strong. In the same way, the tongue is a
small thing that makes grand speeches. But a tiny spark
can set a great forest on fire."

James 3:1–5, NIV

James, or Ya'Akov, is one of my favorite books of the Bible.
Ya'Akov, the brother of Jesus, penned a succinct and practical
guide to daily life. I have spent most of my life as a teacher in
both Sunday School and at a university. As such, Ya'Akov 3:1–5
has always stood out to me. In verse 1, Ya'Akov warns us bluntly.

Ya'Akov goes on through verse 12 warning us about the
tongue. And, in contemporary culture, the tongue is more dan-

gerous simply because we can broadcast our words through social (and unsocial) media. Earlier in Ya'Akov 1:19 he warns us to be "Quick to hear and slow to speak . . .", and those are some of the best words for me to heed. In this era of "instant everything" I, and maybe you, can become terribly impatient. Too often my impatience results in me being "quick to speak and slow to hear . . . ." And, for us teachers, to some extent it is our job to speak, so we are doubly in danger. Maybe that is why Ya'Akov singled us out—well, there's no maybe about it. And, even if you don't carry the title of "teacher" you are still teaching your spouse, and children, and co-workers, and anyone else who spends more than a few minutes with you. Remember, some of Jesus's worst condemnations were for those who were the teachers of the Jewish people.

Ya'Akov's words, applied, can save us a lot of judgment. After all, "sticks and stones can break our bones, and words *can* really hurt us." Think back: you have been hurt with words. And more subtly, you have been hurt by what you have been taught. We were made for community, and we are teaching and learning in many of our interactions, especially those with family and close friends.

So let us pray that G^d will remind us that our tongues can start a forest fire. Let us pray that G^d will remind us of the impact we have on those we love the most. Let's pray that G^d will help us learn to be quick to hear but slow to speak—especially, especially when we are angry (see last part of Jas. 1:19–20).

If you are like me, this need to control my tongue won't be quickly attained. I need to start over again and again—but it will be time well spent. And the more we talk, the more we need to heed these verses.

— **Phillip Bishop**, Exercise Science, University of Alabama

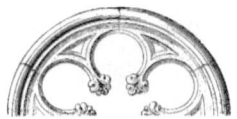

20

Persevering in Prayer

"Then Jesus told them a parable about their need to pray always and not to lose heart. He said, 'In a certain city there was a judge who neither feared God nor had respect for people. In that city there was a widow who kept coming to him and saying, "Grant me justice against my opponent." For a while he refused; but later he said to himself, "Though I have no fear of God and no respect for anyone, yet because this widow keeps bothering me, I will grant her justice, so that she may not wear me out by continually coming."' And the Lord said, 'Listen to what the unjust judge says. And will not God grant justice to his chosen ones who cry to him day and night? Will he delay long in helping them? I tell you, he will quickly grant justice to them. And yet, when the Son of Man comes, will he find faith on earth?'"

Luke 18:1–8, NRSV

T he following story provided an opportunity for me to see faith in action during a mission trip to Haiti with a faculty-student team from our medical school. I believe the Haitians involved had heard the preceding parable and listened to Jesus when he said not to give up.

There was a ten-year-old boy who was a former student at the school in Cité Soleil where our clinic was housed. The child was suffering from an enlarging subcutaneous mass that overlay his windpipe, causing not only cosmetic distress but also progressive obstruction of his airway. His mother was a poor widow and could no longer afford to send him to school, much less pay for medical care, as there is no equivalent to Medicaid in Haiti. Despite all the adversity he faced, this little guy got himself up and dressed each day and came to the school. He watched for us to come out of the clinic building to eat lunch. He would approach us and follow us around, begging not for food but for us to deal with his neck mass. This was not something we could take care of there in an outpatient setting and the child needed to be referred to a surgeon.

Tyler, one of the fourth-year medical students on the team, became the person to whom the little boy came preferentially. Now Tyler was and is a can-do person; he is now a physician in the U.S. Army Medical Corps. He brought funds he had raised from his home church and wanted to pay for the surgery this child needed. When Tyler announced his intentions, the clinic administrator initially balked. What about all the other clinic needs that could be met with that money? Tyler persisted, asking repeatedly to use the money to help that child. Like the widow and the unjust judge, that little boy had come to the clinic every day, asking for help. He connected with Tyler, and Tyler, too, became persistent like the widow. Finally, the clinic administrator agreed to send the child for surgery. Both the little boy and Tyler had faith and did not give up, and God brought about his justice. Their perseverance was an inspiration to all of us on the mission team.

— **Anna Walker**, Medicine, Mercer University

21

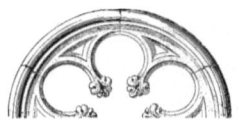

Come Help Change the World

"I will put my Spirit in you and move you to follow my decrees and be careful to keep my laws."

Ezekiel 36:27, NIV

"But I tell you the truth: it is to your advantage that I am leaving; for if I do not leave, the Helper will not come to you; but if I go, I will send Him to you. And He, when He comes, will convict the world regarding sin, and righteousness, and judgment."

John 16:7–8, NIV

To see our world changed, I believe we must rely on the Holy Spirit to do his work in and through us. God has given us the Holy Spirit to empower us to do his work. Jesus said: The Holy Spirit has a huge role in our lives. He opens our eyes to see Christ, brings Christ's words to our memory, and leads us in the direction we should go. As we rely on him, the Holy Spirit can empower us and give us insight into our work as professors, researchers, and writers. As we trust in Christ, the Holy Spirit can do a work in our lives, in our universities, and in our world.

Wouldn't it be wonderful to see a revival in our public universities? I would love to see a move of the Holy Spirit again as in times past. This year I asked the Lord to show up at my university. Then, I co-hosted a prayer meeting where over seventy professors, students, and community leaders came together to pray for the university. I called it "The Jesus Revolution 2 at WWU." Throughout history God has moved in answer to prayer! I love the example of Nehemiah in the Old Testament. Nehemiah, whose name means "Comforter," was living at a time when people really needed comfort. Today, we need God's comfort, hope, and truth.

Much like Nehemiah's time, the spiritual, moral, civil, and social norms in our society have been dismantled, broken down, and obliterated. The Biblical foundations of our public universities have disintegrated. Universities, once founded on God's Word for the formation of students who would carry God's message to their communities and the world, have generally turned away from God. Professors and students need to come together to work and rebuild truth, love, civility, and kindness as the foundation in our universities, communities, and culture. One professor alone cannot do this work. We need an army of people. Nehemiah gives us some steps to follow: First of all, Nehemiah saw the desperate need of his time. Second, Nehemiah went to God in prayer. Third, Nehemiah overcame his fears to go to the king with his concern. Fourth, Nehemiah joined with others to do the work. With God's help, together they rebuilt the wall.

In the midst of the injustice and chaos of the day, we are reminded that God's Holy Spirit is at work in our nation. Recently, he moved at Asbury University and revival broke out. Approximately 15,000 people each day attended the services.

By its end, the revival brought 50,000 to 70,000 visitors representing more than 200 academic institutions and multiple countries. The Holy Spirit also moved at Auburn University, a state-supported institution, where roughly 200 college students gave their lives to Christ and were baptized. The Holy Spirit is at work, and he is at work in us.

Let's consider how we as professors, researchers, and writers, can join with God's work in our universities, in our nation and in the world. How can we work together in the power of the Holy Spirit to proclaim God's Kingdom? We were not placed on earth to build our CV's or our reputations or earn promotions—although God may allow that to happen. Our real purpose here on earth is to be his ambassadors. We represent the King of Kings. Let's consider ways we can allow him to work through us to change our world.

— **Geri Forsberg**, English,
Western Washington University

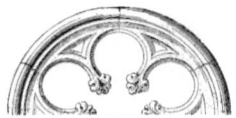

22

A Few Rewards of Teaching

"Now when Jesus came into the region of Caesarea Philippi, He was asking His disciples, 'Who do people say that the Son of Man is?' And they said, 'Some say John the Baptist; and others, Elijah; and still others, Jeremiah, or one of the other prophets.' He said to them, 'But who do you yourselves say that I am?' Simon Peter answered, 'You are the Christ, the Son of the living God.' And Jesus said to him, 'Blessed are you, Simon Barjona, because flesh and blood did not reveal this to you, but My Father who is in heaven. And I also say to you that you are Peter, and upon this rock I will build My church; and the gates of Hades will not overpower it.'"

Matthew 16:13–18, NASB

It is easy for us to get distracted by the things that go wrong in our teaching. If you submit many papers or grant proposals, you know that most reviewers will spend the majority of their review telling you every little thing you did wrong. Often in reviews of our teaching by students or colleagues, our many shortcomings are highlighted. We are often subjected to the negatives of our job, but I'd like to focus on some of the positives.

I fondly remember back in 2010 when that statistics class went so amazingly well for the whole term. Everything clicked, the jokes all worked, the students worked hard and learned much. Years later, I can recall some of those students by name. It would be a good practice to recall some of our most successful classes and thank our Lord for the gift of those moments shared with students.

I recall teaching pedagogy for a group of Afghani university professors in Herat, Afghanistan. I gave a series of 3-hour lectures with translation. I was shocked at how attentive and engaged they were. In that first class I had discussed introverts and extroverts and how to help the introverts contribute to class discussions. Though it happened over 15 years ago, I still recall talking to a student of one of the professors in the class. She came to me in frustration the morning after that first class because her instructor had already over-applied that principle. She related, "Our professor said that we extroverts had to be quiet and let the introverts speak. I want to speak because I am trying to learn the most I can!" I was so grateful to God that he gives the opportunity to teach really enthusiastic, eager students.

In speaking of the rewards of teaching, I have learned that many of us have the same notion of the classic reward in teaching. When I "see the light come on" for a student, I feel God's pleasure. When a student who has previously been confused or disengaged suddenly smiles and begins actively to participate, the classroom is revealed as a sacred space.

I think this is "a light coming on" event we read about in Matthew 16:13–18:

Now when Jesus came into the district of Caesarea Philippi, he asked his disciples, "Who do men say that the Son of Man is?' And they said, 'Some say John the Baptist, others say Elijah, and others Jeremiah or one of the prophets." He said to them, "But who do you say that I am?" Simon Peter replied, "You are the Christ, the Son of the living God." And Jesus answered him, "Blessed are you, Simon Bar-Jona! For flesh and blood has not revealed this to you, but my Father who is in heaven. And I tell you, you are Peter, and on this rock I will build my church, and the powers of death shall not prevail against it."

Over the course of a teaching career, God brings hundreds of students into our classrooms. Many we may not remember, but others will brighten our lives. God gives us many rewards in our teaching, and sometimes "the light comes on" for our students and for us! Let's thank God that we have the privilege of teaching, as well as learning from our students. And let us remember to bless them when the light comes on.

— **Phillip Bishop**, Exercise Science,
   University of Alabama

23

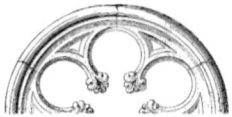

Taking the Lowest Place

"Do nothing from selfish ambition or conceit, but in humility count others more significant than yourselves. Let each of you look not only to his own interests, but also to the interests of others. Have this mind among yourselves, which is yours in Christ Jesus who, though he was in the form of God, did not count equality with God a thing to be grasped, but emptied himself, by taking the form of a servant."

Philippians 2:3; 5–7, ESV

The passage of scripture that has most recently challenged me as a professor comes from Paul's letter to the Philippians. I think about these words when I'm putting on my loafers, buttoning up my coat, and grabbing my coffee to race out the door for my first Penn State advanced writing class of the day. I think about how I can let my life move in one of two directions: full of myself or full of Jesus.

As I drive to campus, I find myself astonished by the counter-cultural commands in Philippians about how Christians ought to conduct themselves. I toss this word "humility" around in my head. Lord, help me be humble! What would this look like today? A humble professor, if I apply Paul's words, *looks to the interests of her students and colleagues, becomes like a servant to them*, and *speaks with joyful, peaceful words*. In other words, I want to care about students' lives, serve them, and rejoice in the Lord in their presence.

This way of being contrasts with my self-promoting, self-involved, complaining nature. Would I allow the Holy Spirit to make me more like Jesus? Could I die to myself and think of practical ways to live out Philippians 2? I park my car, brace myself against the cold morning air, and picture the day ahead of teaching, faculty meetings, and office hour conversations with students and professors who stop by.

A wise mentor once told me her summary of Philippians 2: *Take the lowest place.* Taking the lowest place in any setting means I'm looking for ways to serve (prompt email replies and returned grades, writing recommendations, coaching students on professional development), to do the tasks others don't want to do in meetings (set agendas, make copies, bring snacks), and to honor others above myself (compliment strengths and notice accomplishments). I resist the temptation toward anger or annoyance when students ask for accommodation, for more office-hour help, for last-minute recommendations, or for extensions on projects. Taking the lowest place would mean giving preferential treatment to everyone around me, rejoicing always, and not stirring up controversy with department gossip.

Another mentor told me her summary of every great leadership skill she's ever learned: be helpful.

That's it. Be helpful.

In any setting, I can *be helpful*. Living out Philippians 2 connects me to Jesus and the ways he took on the nature of servant.

I want to reflect this about him every day on campus. As I walk to my classroom, I pray, "Jesus, make me more like you as you took on the nature of a servant. Help me ask good questions to learn about my students, to take on their interests and care about their lives. Help me speak with joyful words. Help me take the lowest place like you did."

— **Heather Holleman**, English,
Pennsylvania State University

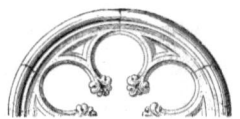

24

Who's Witnessing to Whom?

"Now faith is confidence in what we hope for and assurance about what we do not see."

Hebrews 11:1, NIV

I am a pathologist and have spent nearly 40 years teaching mechanisms of disease and laboratory medicine to medical students. During the latter part of my career, some students were kind enough to invite me to accompany them on a medical mission trip to Mexico. That led to my participating in mission trips to Haiti over the following five years. Although I am not a primary care provider, I was able to support the clinicians on our team by providing point of care laboratory testing. Why did we go? Well, we liked to think that we brought some help to the people we treated, but I am more inclined to think that we were the ones who learned and benefited from those people we met. Meeting them made me reflect on my life, my faith, my teaching, and on life in general here in America.

Our clinic was in Cité Soleil, which is a region in Port-au-Prince of abject poverty. Open sewers run down the middle of dirt streets. Piles of garbage are everywhere. Goats, chickens, a few very thin cows wander around. Homes are small squat concrete structures with no electricity or running water.

On Sunday we attended a church in Cité Soleil where the pastor in charge of our host school was preaching. Everyone was dressed up—coats and ties for men, dresses for ladies—and looked very nice. Along the aisles were monitors who were very stern-looking women. They determined if congregants were dressed appropriately and oversaw behavior throughout the service. No one could stretch out an arm on the bench behind someone else, as this might have been interpreted as a public display of affection.

The sermon and service were in Haitian Creole. I could not follow it, but there was a very nice interpreter sitting next to me. He was a teacher, about 30 years old, and very polite. During lulls in the service, he would ask me questions about America. One question I remember was about religion in the U.S. I told him that many people considered themselves Christian, that there were Catholics and evangelicals like in Haiti and also Jews, Muslims, Buddhists, Hindus, and other faiths. He was familiar with all of these. Then I told him that there were also people of no faith. That caught him by surprise. He said he had never contemplated the concept of having no faith, of not believing in God. And the way he talked about it, it was apparent that his amazement came not only from his personal belief in God, but also that he could not believe anyone would deny God existed. He had literally never met a nonbeliever.

Now, one might say that was because people were afraid to admit their lack of belief. Obviously, there were those strict monitors overseeing the congregation. Haiti, however, had limited law and order presiding over anything else. (I saw one traffic light the whole time I was there.) So there were definitely no religious police who would know whether one went to church or who would listen to conversations outside of the sanctuary. No one was going to report a nonbeliever to some kind of authority. Also, if there were any place on the planet that one might consider describing as "godforsaken," it was Cité Soleil with its hovels and garbage and sewage and smells. Nonetheless, the people there had great faith. They were demonstrably grateful to God. They rejoiced in the fellowship they had with each other. Despite all the unfortunate things that had happened in Haiti, the people did not seem to despair.

I have thought about this young man and his genuine surprise at how anyone could be lacking in faith. What is it about our American society that fosters unbelief? We all have so much material wealth compared to almost all Haitians and so much opportunity. One would think we would all be thanking and praising God at all times. Maybe the Haitians should be doing mission work among us.

— **Anna N. Walker**, Medicine, Mercer University

25

The Devotional Life for Followers of Jesus

"Martha, Martha, you are worried and bothered about so many things; but only one thing is necessary, for Mary has chosen the good part, which shall not be taken away from her."

Luke 10:41–42, NASB

Without doubt, the most significant lesson I've learned in my Christian walk came from Jesus through Mary of Bethany, the sister of Lazarus and Martha. As you will recall, when Martha complained to the Master that her sister Mary was not helping prepare the meal, Jesus gave the above-quoted response.

Jesus's response here has profound implications for his followers, yet I suspect that most believers who read this narrative miss the point. What is Jesus really saying here? The fact that Jesus called Martha's name twice indicates that he is trying to break through her distraction and focus her on what he is going to say to her next.

Then he states this absolutely remarkable principle, "There

is really only one thing necessary in life—to know Me, to hear My word, to be in My presence. Mary has discovered this. I am not going to tell Mary to stop doing the only truly necessary thing in life—spending time in My presence—to do something else that, while it may seem important to you, is in the grand scheme of things really trivial" (my paraphrase of Matthew 10:41–42). Jesus tells the sisters, and us too, if we will listen, that the only necessary activity for us as his followers is to spend time with him.

Do you realize that the only thing preventing you from having an effective devotional life may be you? That's right—you. Do you believe that meeting with the Lord in his word should be the most important activity of your day? Whether we like it or not, the way we spend our time is the best measure of our priorities. If we have time for our job, time for our family, time for hobbies but no time for the Lord we must seriously question whether our job, family, or hobbies are more important than the Lord.

If we love the Lord the way he commands us to in Matthew 22:35–38, with all our heart, soul, and mind, then we will make time to spend with him, to get to know him. The first step in having an effective devotional life is to determine to make fellowship with the Lord the priority of our lives. Then we will set aside time to spend with him.

I first started considering these ideas 25 or more years ago. After much reflection, I had to admit spending time with Jesus was not the priority of my life but I could make it the top priority of every single day. Since I decided to take that step, the Lord has blessed me more than words could ever say, and the relationship I have with him because of this simple decision is profoundly satisfying.

I am convinced that our devotional times cultivate our relationship with Jesus. This makes the difference between just understanding the facts of Christianity and having a vital, dynamic relationship with the Lord of the universe. We are invited to understand his plans and be involved in his work in his Creation.

Knowing God in a new and deeper way, I increasingly wanted to share this knowledge with my students and colleagues. I began offering an optional class session in which I addressed the questions "Who am I?", "Why am I here?", and "Where am I going?" Over the years in these sessions, I shared my life story with scores of students—typically 70% of undergraduates and 95% of graduate students in my classes attended the optional class. For faculty colleagues, I published a book, *Ministering in the Secular University*, in which I shared ideas that have been used by Christian professors and staff to reach out to colleagues and students with the Good News about our Lord Jesus.[17] This book is widely used to communicate the only truly necessary thing in life.

— **Joseph McRae Mellichamp**, Management Science, University of Alabama

26

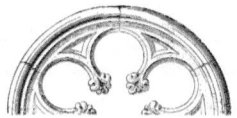

The Eyes of the Heart

"I pray that the eyes of your heart may be enlightened in order that you may know the hope to which he has called you."

Ephesians 1:18a, NIV

Scripture tells us that unless we become like children, we shall not enter the kingdom of God (Matt. 18:3); however, St. Paul counsels that, as we age, we need to set aside childish thinking (1 Cor. 13:11). Confusing? Well, not really, though the subtlety of this contrast enables us to understand why some educators find the thought of initiating children into the Christian faith a very challenging task, especially since too many youths never grow up to follow St. Paul's command to think maturely about their faith.

My personal faith journey began when I received a Catholic baptism a few months after my birth, though my real introduction to the Christian faith and scripture came when my parents sent me as a child to Bible school at a Methodist Church around the corner from our home. There I learned the simple, child-appropriate meaning of Jesus's parables, and this early Christian educational experience was a real "pearl of great price" (Matt. 13:46) that I've treasured my whole life.

When my parents returned to Catholicism years later, they naturally brought their teen-aged children with them. My high school catechism classes lacked substance, progressively birthing a desire for a mature Catholic education. I purposefully chose to attend a Catholic university. In my very first semester, my dynamic Jesuit theology professor challenged us to think about the *objective* reality of the "being" to whom we prayed: who was this "Our Father," really? Although I did not anticipate that this question would throw me into a theological tailspin of onto-logical doubt, I did realize that the answer to this philosophical question would undergird my sincere, but still maturing faith. Thus, my freshman year turned into a prolonged metaphysical search for a rational solution to this very fundamental question: can humans know, not just believe, that this Creator God truly exists? Surprisingly, and despite my many months of hard think-ing, God answered this speculative question in His own very unexpected way; instead of working through my mind, God opened "the eyes of my heart" (Eph. 1:18).

On a late spring morning, I sat quietly on a garden bench. Opposite me was an enormous, weathered magnolia tree with huge magenta blossoms framed by an intense blue sky. Intellec-tually exhausted, I let my guard down . . . and boom! suddenly, beauty knocked me off my thought-obsessed horse, and just like that, I realized I was in the unmistakable presence of the Holy (Exod. 3:5)! As my soul whispered the familiar words, "poems are made by fools like me, but only God can make a tree," my heart yearned to share this sacred aesthetic encounter with everyone I loved.[18] In my moment of profound spiritual vulnerability, God enlightened the eyes of my heart and this affective experience trumped all of my sustained mental labors (Eph. 1:18–23). I now saw clearly that this Creator God made *all* things out of the generous superabundance of his creative Love, and through my simple intuition of his divine name, Beauty, my heart and life were irrevocably transformed (Eccl. 3:11).

Dramatic changes followed quickly. Inspired by the aesthetics of Thomist philosopher, Jacques Maritain, I changed my major to philosophy. Then God, through his own good grace and at his own prudent pace, led me to understand the three rational "Preambles of Faith" articulated by the Catholic Intellectual Tradition, and these subtle distinctions anchored my blossoming faith. No longer in intellectual despair, I now saw clearly how God had used the grandeur and beauty of a simple magnolia tree to awaken me to the sacred, spiritual dimension of his magnificent creation (Jer. 29:13).

As an adult I became eager to serve him. I eventually became a Christian professor of philosophy with one main goal: regardless of anything they learned in class, I wanted my students to use the eyes of their hearts and see God's gifts of Beauty and Love through a spiritual lens, so that they too, like the Apostles Peter, James, and John at Jesus's Transfiguration, might be transformed and say: "Lord, it is good that we are here!" (Matt. 17:4).

— **John G. Trapani Jr.**, Philosophy, Walsh University

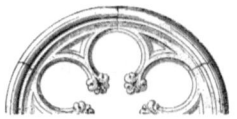

27

Today

> "So God set another time for entering his rest and that time is today. God *announced* this through David much later. . . *'Today* when you hear his voice, don't harden your hearts.'"
>
> Hebrews 4:7, NLT, emphasis added

In Numbers 13–14, the Israelites are afraid to enter Canaan when the spies sent by Moses return with 10 negative reports to only two encouraging ones by Joshua and Caleb. The writer of Hebrews refers to the lesson of that failure in the above-cited passage.

During my sophomore year in college, my French professor Wallace Fowlie assigned us a poem by the symbolist poet Stéphane Mallarmé. It was not a long text, just a sonnet, but it was, like just about all Mallarmé's poems, extremely dense and opaque for my untutored brain. It tells the story of a swan who is caught in a frozen lake and can't escape. He has failed to take wing until it's too late. The poem's first word is *"Aujourd'hui/* Today," and it gradually becomes clear that the swan is the symbol for Today. Professor Fowlie that day proceeded to guide us through that poem with such astonishing insight that it was like a beautiful flower opening to the sunlight. Professor Fowlie's lecture that morning was for me a memorable epiphany. It was, in retrospect, the birth of my vocation as a professor.

The swan's inertia when it failed to take flight during the season of migration caused it to end up in the death-throes of a frozen landscape. What a tragedy! The poet himself was paralyzed by his fear of failure but ultimately managed to overcome his dread of the blank page symbolized by the frozen lake and take wing on poetic inspiration. The ten spies with negative reports were also defeated by their fears, and they paid for their inaction by wandering for years in the desert rather than entering into their promised destiny. Joshua and Caleb like the poet in Mallarmé's sonnet were willing to "seize the day," and they were eventually permitted to enter into the Promised Land of milk and honey.

I've reread and taught that poem many times and it still makes today come alive in all its possibilities.

We professors seldom have any idea what impact we're having on a given student in a given class. However, each new day of the semester is an opportunity to ignite a similar epiphany in some questing spirit. We should prepare our classes prayerfully and ask for sensitivity to know when we have an opportunity to be more than an instructor. The Master Teacher can guide us as we follow him.

Wallace Fowlie became much more than an instructor to me. Because of his kindness and the personal interest he took in me, I thank God even *today* for his beneficent influence and his loyal friendship.

"His merciful love couldn't have dried up. They're created new every morning." (Lamentations 3:22, MSG)

— **John Marson Dunaway**, French and
Interdisciplinary Studies, Mercer University

28

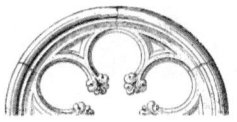

Summoned

"Before I formed you in the womb I knew you, before you were born I set you apart; I appointed you as a prophet to the nations."

Jeremiah 1:5, NIV

"And it was at that age . . . Poetry arrived / in search of me."[19]

Pablo Neruda

"*Find your passion*": The average young adult has heard these words numerous times. But how do young people "find their passion"? How do they discover their purpose or calling? While one's passion can be found, one's calling or vocation needs to be *heard*.

Parker Palmer speaks of one stage of his vocational journey as "something that I can't not do."[20] But what does the voice of calling sound like and where does it come from?

This is the dilemma that Pablo Neruda faced. He could not tell how or when he heard the call to poetry. There were no voices, there were no words, neither was it silence. But yet he was summoned.

As I reflect on this poem, I ponder what it means to summon or be summoned. It is a form of awakening that arrives as a result of newly acquired consciousness.

One purpose of a teacher's calling is to help in the "summoning" of students to their call. As an important voice in the world of our students, college professors can participate in summoning students to their calling or vocation. Young people need help in the journey of discovering purpose from clergy, mentors, coaches, or guides who have personal knowledge of them.

Facilitating our students' search for their vocation does not mean telling them what we think they should major in or do with their lives. It entails being attentive to them and being ready and willing to point them in the right direction. This can take the form of bearing witness to what is already in them but may not be evident to them. It can include highlighting their gifts and talents and motivating them to explore new areas of personal growth and curiosity.

I recently led a short-term study-abroad trip to Portugal to study the health implications of migration and displacement on refugees and immigrants. A very talented young lady whom I had mentored through a student newsletter team was excited to enroll in the class. Having never traveled abroad, she was enthusiastic but apprehensive. I learned that she was interested in a career in refugee resettlement. Although it appeared she had made up her mind about her career choice, she still needed strong confirmation that this was what she should be doing with her life.

The trip delivered everything she needed for this final confirmation. On the second day, she shared with the entire group that her encounters the previous day had confirmed all the reasons she desired a career in refugee resettlement. On the fourth day, while helping to serve a community dinner to recent migrants, she received a job offer from a refugee resettlement agency in the U.S. She remembers I said these words to her upon hearing the news: "This trip has been so serendipitous, everything came together for you to receive this news in this place." While I may not have helped her identify her specific calling to serve refugees, I am grateful that by serving in my vocation, I was able to support the development of her gift of writing and design a program whose timing and content were instrumental in helping her confirm the vocational direction to which she felt summoned.

Jesus provides a perfect example of how to participate in the summoning of people to their calling and vocation. All his disciples (students) were literally "summoned" to their calling by him. He employed intentional pedagogical practices that succeeded in setting a "fire" in their souls and propelled them to hear and walk in their calling. Some of the features of his pedagogy include the following:

1. His lectures contained many stories and parables.
2. He got to know his students at a personal level.
3. He used interactive teaching approaches, often starting with questions.

By thus helping students discover their vocation, we contribute to God's kingdom agenda.

— **Chinekwu Obidoa,** Global Health,
Mercer University

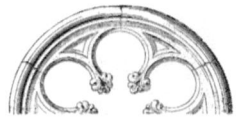

29

Married to Truth

"Ye shall know the truth, and the truth shall make
you free."

John 8:33, KJV

"What is truth?" asked Pilate, unaware that Truth was standing before him in the flesh. The contemporary American university proclaims itself to be in pursuit of truth, but all too often scholars are only after knowledge. Many even join in Pilate's post-modern style question in their deconstructive diatribes against what they view as empty metanarratives about "meaning." One of the keys that Jesus gave us to growing in truth is found in John 7:17 (NASB): "If anyone is willing to do His will, he will know of the teaching, whether it is of God or whether I speak from Myself." Which is why the Psalmist says, "I understand more than the ancients, because I keep thy precepts" (Ps. 119:100, KJV). Obedience to truth opens the way to new dimensions of revelation, or a *rhema* word.

Knowledge is something scholars can master and use for their own ends, whereas truth is something (or someone) to be served. Dr. Dennis Kinlaw writes that "There is an element of unrelenting moral demand in truth; it is other-centered. It matters not whether we have mastered truth and can use it; it matters only if we have surrendered to truth and are willing to obey it." Kinlaw adds, "Someone has suggested that truth is like a potential spouse who to be known truly demands of us commitment and a pledge of undying fidelity."[21]

As a twenty-something rookie assistant professor of French, I was constantly afraid of making grammatical errors in class, particularly when writing on the chalkboard (yes, I go back that far!). That kind of fear can paralyze a teacher, particularly when teaching a foreign language as a non-native. I found a measure of freedom from that paralysis when a colleague in a pedagogical discussion talked about what a "teachable moment" it can be when we're caught in a mistake in the classroom.

I once invited two speakers to a class to address the opposite sides of an extremely controversial topic. Their exchange became so heated that they literally almost came to blows. That class was a failure. It was destructive to the fabric of academic inquiry, and I determined never again to invite opposing sides on the same day. Debates are too often designed for competition, not mutual civility and understanding.

Psychologists tell us the one thing children most want to hear their parents say is, "I was wrong." It's disarming. Students, too, tend to feel increasing respect for teachers who admit their failings in front of the class. A teacher shows wisdom in establishing an atmosphere for classroom discussions in which truth (rather than solely knowledge) is the center toward which we all strive. While the teacher does indeed retain pedagogical authority, her function is not simply to impart knowledge. And a discussion should never become a debate about who is wrong and who is right. The most positive conversations in my classes occur when everyone—teacher and students—know that to be gently and respectfully corrected by another is a gift, a win-win proposition. Humility in serving the truth is the key. An effective teacher is one who is "married" to Truth and serves the one who said, "I am the truth," having "pledged undying fidelity."

"I am the way, the truth, and the life." (John 14:6, KJV)

— **John Marson Dunaway**, French and
  Interdisciplinary Studies, Mercer University

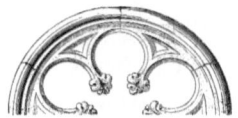

30

Education and Priorities

"For what is a man profited, if he shall gain the whole
world, and lose his own soul? Or what shall a man give in
exchange for his soul?"

Matthew 16:26, KJV

Jesus is recorded as giving his own "graduate students" the
above-cited very useful advice. Many of our students are focused on earning their degree, whichever one it may be. True,
they may often forget the broader purposes of a university education, but eventually most of them remember that they are
in school to build a résumé for a decent job. Sadly, though, all
too many, in the process of gaining their degree, forfeit their
own soul. Quite often, students who come into the university
with a firm grasp of their Christian heritage and beliefs fall
victim to the "spirit of the age." Their highly educated, sometimes hostile-to-Christianity, professors either subtly or overtly
attack their Christian foundations. These attacks, coupled with
the many temptations of the flesh, cause many to stray from the
faith. Some will eventually return to their faith, but others are
forfeiting their souls!

So what can we Christian professors do about this tragic loss of souls? We can take every opportunity to be salt and light for our students. We can mention before class what we are studying in the Bible (arriving early in order to chat with students is an excellent practice). We can offer to pray for students if they encounter difficulties. We can bring a Bible to class, not to read it there, but to provoke questions. If we are brave enough, we can tell them we are Followers of the Christ (a more meaningful title these days than "Christian"). We can even tell them we love them. Think about it—you probably do love them, and they are yearning to be loved by someone these days.

For students from previous terms, whom we no longer have in class, we can take them to lunch and ask them about their religious upbringing and current beliefs. We might even ask them about their souls—how are they doing? We could share our own journey of faith.

I clearly recall one of my doctoral students who came to me after completing his undergraduate degrees under one of my former PhD students. "Sam" had grown up in such a dysfunctional home that he moved out on his own at age 15. Sam came to our university, found a relationship with Jesus and was rapidly growing as a disciple. He was so enjoying being a follower of the Christ that when he finished his master's he stayed for a PhD. When he finished his dissertation, he was reluctant to take the next step into professional life. The secure little world of graduate study with opportunities for Christian fellowship was too comfortable for him to leave. I was able to convince him that God could continue to grow him in his new role as a professor and God has been faithful.

Sam is indeed a rare case, but he demonstrates that students, even graduate students, can grow in Christ as they grow academically. Let us think about who among our students might come to Christ or grow in him. There's no end to things that could be done, but perhaps the most important thing is for us to realize that there are souls at stake, eternal souls.

Lord, increase our faith, increase our boldness, increase our love for these souls that are perishing. Lord, help us teach with a constant awareness of the souls of our students.

— **Phillip Bishop**, Exercise Science,
University of Alabama

31

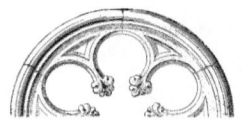

May the Words

"May the words of my mouth and the meditations of my heart be acceptable in thy sight, O Lord my strength and my redeemer."

Psalm 19:14, KJV

"There are probably words addressed to our condition exactly, which, if we could really hear and understand, would be more salutary than the morning . . . ."[22]

Henry David Thoreau

The above-quoted scripture is one translation of a sentence within one of David's psalms. It is almost always said as a petitionary prayer by priests or pastors just before they begin their sermons. Some thirty or so years ago, this struck me as a strange limitation and I started saying these words to myself as an experimental discipline before every class, every seminar, every paper presentation, and every panel discussion. This then is my phenomenological report to you of the experience of doing this, offered so that you may consider if it is fitting for you as a teacher.

"May the words . . ." Initially these words were just

reassuring, surprisingly calming, pulling me away from the stage fright that is a way of life for teachers. How odd this is! How odd that asking for the judgment of all that is divine upon one's words would be calming. But it was. And in being so it let me know that the judgment I was requesting would always be delivered as love.

"May the words . . ." First I thought that perhaps this calming was because the words reminded me of who the true audience was, and thus offered an escape from the unfathomable complexities, difficulties, incompleteness, and disappointments of all human relations, but this was a very serious theological error, one separating the Divine from those who were before me as an audience when, in fact, they were inseparable.

"May the words . . ." After many years, I noticed, or perhaps this noticed me, that the "words of my mouth" were not to be separated from the "meditations of my heart", that is, that I was implicitly offering to be one in what I was doing. There was to be in this no separation between role and self, for self was known and made whole in role and role was known and made whole in self, and neither could be separated from the other for the division would make honesty before the Divine, who clearly does not tolerate such division, impossible. King David knew this.

"May the words . . ." Sometimes the words, at their dearest, worked like a clearing in the deep forest that one stumbles into along a dark trail. Those classes, those seminars, those presentations, those panels, were my favorites, the ones where I could honestly wonder, as some artists do, from where my own words had come, a certain sense of things falling into place, and, in this, a fittingness, a meaning I could not have imagined on my own. And for these I was grateful, for I knew that these were gifts.

"May the words . . ." Later, listening to this psalm read one day at church, it dawned on me that when David said these words he said them not at the beginning but at the end of a song of praise. They seem to mean for him something like: "I hope my song was pleasing," and they seemed almost disingenuous like the letters of Bach that accompanied his gift of a piece to a royal patron. There was nothing of a petition in David's use of the prayer nor was there—and this had seemed to me to be the most natural use of the prayer—a humbling of oneself before God, as Augustine would have us do, as a prelude to having the audacity to speak.

"May the words . . ." Perhaps, I thought, there is something profound in this difference; something about the nature of the relationship we can have with that which is divine in our time as opposed to David's. The prayer, as I was using it, singled out an event for particular attention and, when it worked as I described above, it was its working in that moment that seemed a gift and one for which gratitude was owed. But why this limitation? Why this attention to these events, to these moments?

"May the words . . ." "Why do you approach the Divine so obliquely?" the words seem to ask of me. "Why is your most typical experience of it so ephemeral? Why is its infinite beauty so fleeting to your perceptions?" Perhaps it is because it is too obvious to be noticed, the words suggested as an answer to its own questions, like the water in which the fish does not know it is swimming.

"May the words . . ." So the words, while retaining for me all that they had offered before, also became for me that which had preceded them in David's song of praise: each a reminder of a constant presence there with us like the sun, for:

The heavens declare the glory of God; and the firmament sheweth his handywork. Day unto day uttereth speech, and night unto night sheweth knowledge. There is no speech nor language, where their voice is not heard. Their line is gone out through all the earth, and their words to the end of the world. In them hath he set a tabernacle for the sun, Which is as a bridegroom coming out of his chamber, and rejoiceth as a strong man to run a race. His going forth is from the end of the heaven, and his circuit unto the ends of it: and there is nothing hid from the heat thereof. (Psalm 19:14, NKJV)

And they became "more salutary than morning."

— **Jack L. Sammons**, Law, Mercer University

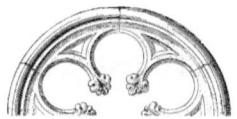

32

Under the Gaze of Jesus:
A Tribute to Jean-Louis Chrétien

"For if you listen to the word and don't obey, it is like glancing at your face in a mirror. You see yourself, walk away, and forget what you look like."

James 1:23–24, NLT

In June of 2008 I was in northern Senegal with a group of Mercer students. We had to pack lightly and near the end of the 23 days in country I found myself running out of reading materials. In the old colonial capital of Saint-Louis I found a newsstand and bought the current copy of the French weekly *Le Figaro Magazine* and read it cover to cover. The jewel I discovered in that periodical was a review of Jean-Louis Chrétien's new book on reading scripture, *Sous le regard de la Bible/Under the Gaze of the Bible*. I had never even heard of Chrétien, but when I read that article, I knew I had found a rich source of spiritual and intellectual nourishment.

Chrétien (born 1952 in Paris) was a professor of philosophy at the Sorbonne and a prolific writer. He published not only scholarly works on ancient and medieval philosophy, but he was a poet and literary critic as well. He was described as fitting into a group of writers referred to as representing a "theological turn in French phenomenology."

As soon as I got home from Senegal, I ordered Chrétien's book and eagerly read it. I was dazzled by his intellect, moved to tears by the beauty of the writing, and surprised to find how ecumenical this Roman Catholic's theology was, quoting Barth, Luther, or Calvin as often as Origen and Augustine.

During my next sabbatical leave in Paris, I went to his office at the Sorbonne and stationed myself at the end of the line of grad students waiting to see him. I had taken a cue from a colleague who tried showing up unannounced at a Sorbonne professor's office, and it worked! The students raved about his kindness in spending so much time with them during his office hours. They obviously were drawn to him by his gentle demeanor, a kindness that was buttressed by his brilliance and an intellectual passion for truth.

After the students had visited, he greeted me warmly and we had a wonderful conversation. I was delighted when he agreed to allow me to translate his book, which had meant so much to me. I was blessed to meet with him on several subsequent occasions over café au lait or a glass of wine when I was in Paris.

Under the Gaze of the Bible is a treasure for those who love God's word. Chrétien gives his readers many rich insights. The title gives us the main thesis, namely, that, ideally, believers should actually strive to allow the Bible to read us! It is the mirror that James refers to in the verse printed at the beginning of this meditation.

Though Chrétien's parents were agnostics and he had no religious upbringing, he came to faith through his philosophy studies, which should not come as a surprise to us. "Anyone, after all, who seeks earnestly for truth must in the end find Jesus," he once remarked to me, speaking of his journey to faith.

Chrétien was a man who knew his calling. He steadfastly refused invitations to join the lecture circuit and shunned the media. Instead, he was totally dedicated to teaching and mentoring his students in their philosophical and theological studies, and to a demanding regimen of writing books that will continue to guide us in our pursuit of "faith seeking understanding."

My friend Jean-Louis Chrétien died on June 28, 2019, at the age of 66, just a year after his retirement. He had run the good race, and he now sits under the gaze of his Lord. I miss him, but I do look forward to a warm reunion with him in glory!

> "Thy statutes have been my song in the house of my pilgrimage." (Ps. 119:54, KJV)

— **John Marson Dunaway**, French and
  Interdisciplinary Studies, Mercer University

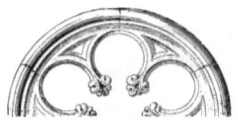

33

Teaching as Annunciation

"Do not be afraid, Mary, for you have found favor
with God."

Luke 1:30, AMP

Following a trip to Egypt and Palestine, Henry Ossawa Tanner painted *The Annunciation* in 1897.[23]

At the age of thirteen Tanner decided he wanted to be a painter, dismissing his father's hopes that he would become a minister in the African Methodist Episcopal Church. Benjamin Tucker Tanner was himself a pastor in the AME church and an abolitionist in the Jim Crow era. Henry Tanner's mother Sarah Elizabeth Miller Tanner was a slave who found her way to freedom on the Underground Railroad. From this inheritance, responding to an inner annunciation, Henry Ossawa Tanner became the first successful African American painter in an art world predominantly white.

The angel Gabriel's visitation to a young peasant Mary informing her that in her womb she would carry the Christ child was not simply an affirmation of her belovedness; it also symbolizes the reality that all human beings are dwelling places for the *imago dei* to be lived in our human experiences. For African slaves and their descendants, annunciation released the harbored hope of freedom arising from an inner trust in their own belovedness.

Those called to teach—in the natural and social sciences, humanities, music, and the arts, in classrooms, or through research—have likely responded to annunciations carried across generations in their bodies and psyches or perhaps awakened by observant others. Learning to watch and to listen for annunciations inwardly and outwardly, to wrestle with them, and then to be attentive and responsive are our daily human assignments: to embrace our belovedness and to develop and refine our capacity for *holy presence.*

When we enter our personal cells of contemplation or the classrooms of waiting students, may we become attentive Gabriels announcing the good news of belovedness to the deeply listening souls of our students and ourselves. Entered with reverence and anticipation, the classroom becomes sacred space for the Holy Spirit's transformations.

Listening for Annunciation
By Ruthann Knechel Johansen

Advent is waiting time,
walking expectantly,
peering into houses,
or alleys and cathedrals,

gazing endlessly at lists
hoping—for the origin story
to wrap us round again
in angel wings and fleece.

On this dark December night
far from the first announcement,
words and music will
proclaim again the Mystery.

A painted image,
icon telling of the past,
reveals a Jewish peasant's
rumpled wrestling with a visitation.

In her flesh we see/know our own.

Ah, tonight let's not hide
in what happened
long ago. Let us wait
still. Listen. Watch

for Light streaming
into our peasant bedrooms,
our barren, anxious hearts.

Announced again,
a new quickening of Love
waiting to be birthed
into our midst.[24]

— **Ruthann Knechel Johansen**,
    Professor Emerita, University of Notre Dame,
    President Emerita, Bethany Theological Seminary

34

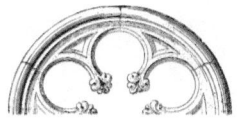

Seasons of the Soul

"Lift up your heads, O ye gates; and be ye lift up, ye everlasting doors; and the King of glory shall come in."

Psalm 24:7, KJV

During the long last weeks of fall semester, we professors sometimes get a bit bogged down by all the papers to be graded and committee work to be completed . . . not to mention the rejection notices one often receives from submissions of scholarly work or grant applications.

Sometimes my devotional life, too, gets similarly caught in the dryness of routine and I'm not sure where to turn for inspiration. Should I start rereading the Psalms? Get a new devotional book? Change my habits of prayer?

We are told in Scripture to "lift up your heads, for your redemption draweth nigh" (Luke 21:28, KJV). That is certainly the heart of the Advent message. One of the things about Advent and Christmas that I love the most is that it renews my expectancy about God's active, albeit hidden, participation in my own life and in events all around me. I remind myself that he is orchestrating it all for his purposes and for my ultimate good, as in Romans

8:28. These reflections may come to us as we watch the Advent candles being lighted at our worship services and contemplate the awesome mystery of the incarnation. We may also think of how the Virgin Mary passed the long, lonely months between the Annunciation and the Nativity awaiting her Savior's birth. Great expectations are indeed appropriate during this season!

I'm grateful for the change of seasons that brings me cozy warmth or refreshing coolness, the rebirth of nature in spring, the blazing color of fall, and even the special beauty of the gray bare woods in winter when I gaze out my window and watch the sun rise between those darkened tree trunks. How much more grateful I am for the "seasons of the soul," as Christian poet Allen Tate called them.[25] Grateful that the dry, arid days of humdrum routine are always followed by the promise of renewal: "Christ in you, the hope of glory" (Col. 1:27, KJV). It's a reflection of God's promise of eternal glory with him that Advent comes in "the bleak midwinter," as Christina Rosetti's poem has it. The Holy Virgin's expectant wait was the prelude to an unimaginable spectacle:

Angels and archangels may have gathered there,
Cherubim and seraphim thronged the air;
But His mother only, in her maiden bliss,
Worshipped the Beloved with a kiss.[26]

Rosetti's poem is our answer to Mark Lowry's rhetorical questions in his own song about the young Virgin with Child, "Mary, Did You Know?"[27] Lowry asks the Virgin if she knows the son she has delivered will soon deliver her. He adds that when she kisses the baby's face, she is kissing, in effect, her own Creator. What an ineffably beautiful mystery!

When we're burdened with the busy-work of grading, committee assignments, or some monotonous research task, we can remind ourselves that the Holy Spirit is still at work in every aspect of our lives, even in these circumstances of the teaching life. "Work out your own salvation with fear and trembling, for it is God which worketh in you both to will and to do of his good pleasure" (Phil. 2:12–13, KJV).

Lift up your heads, o ye academic gates, that the King of Glory may come in! Oh, come, oh, come, Emmanuel! *Maranatha*!

— **John Marson Dunaway**, French and
    Interdisciplinary Studies, Mercer University

35

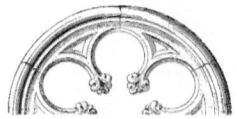

Knowing Them By Name

"My sheep hear my voice, and I know them, and they follow me."

John 10:27, KJV

A s was our custom, we invited a new faculty member and his wife to dinner, welcoming them to our Honors College. He was fresh from his doctoral defense, but several weeks into his first term of teaching he was proving already to be popular with his students, who spoke of his sparkling lectures and spritely manner. As we were finishing dessert, he turned the conversation to his own aspirations as a young professional. He wanted advice.

"You are nearing the end of your long and productive career," he said. "What advice would you give me for mine?" I am not sure what he expected, but he was clearly taken aback somewhat by my answer. "Pray for your students daily, each by name," I said.

"How do you find time to do that?" he asked. "In my case," I answered, "I do it on my way into the university in the morning. I start as soon as I get my class lists and I find it not only

135

helps me learn their names more quickly, but it focuses me on my teaching of them individually, not just as the group in GTX 2302, section four."

My young colleague mumbled something to the effect that he found my practice interesting and would consider it. I am not sure whether he did it or not.

I have often had colleagues, many of them more senior, ask me how I manage not only to remember my students' names, but also, years afterward, to retain considerable details about their lives, backgrounds, parents, and sometimes life trials and tribulations. The answer I give is always the one I gave to my new first-year colleague that evening.

Since my calamitous, over-thick and content-driven first year of teaching, I have come to realize that the calling of a teacher is less about the teaching of books or methods than it is about the persons one is teaching. Rather than addressing the class collectively only, I keep eye contact with individual students in the class as I teach, being especially careful to "read" now and then the eyes of quieter students and those whom I suspect or know to be facing struggles, perhaps not just in my own class. This helps me serve them better, even guiding them in topics for their papers. Often, I have seen pain in young eyes which alerted me to deeper troubles, and I have been able to get those students help.

Most of my students come to my office more than once in a semester. They invariably have an academic question related to the course or to their shaping of coursework toward graduation and whatever they hope follows. But there is often a deeper question behind the ostensible question that brought them to my office door. The conversations which follow build relation-ships, and I have much evidence that their value is retained long after much of the curriculum content has vanished from their memories.

Perhaps the best practice for any of us who are Christian teachers would be to imitate as much as possible the teaching manner of Jesus. While I jokingly refer to my own style as "sheep-dogging," what I have in mind is a conception of my calling as to be a kind of sub-shepherd, and I can find no better guidance than the Lord's example and his words. I am thinking here of his repeated references to shepherds, good and bad, but especially to his saying, "My sheep hear my voice, and I know them, and they follow me" (John 10:27, KJV).

We ought not to seek to make disciples for ourselves—we are far too fallible for that. But we ought, by word and example, to play our part in making disciples for our Lord. If we are to have a chance of doing that, we need first to get to know the "sheep" under our care. They all hear our voices—some of them well enough to imitate us in the cafeteria. Praying for each one daily quickens our ability to know them, and thus to teach them more effectively.

— **David Lyle Jeffrey**, Literature and Humanities, Baylor University

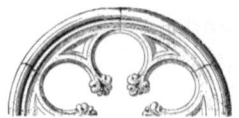

36

Seeing God's Glory

"In the year that king Uzziah died I saw also the Lord sitting upon a throne, high and lifted up, and his train filled the temple."

Isaiah 6:1, KJV

I'm sure I'm not alone. I spent as much time completing my bachelors, masters, and doctoral degrees as I did completing kindergarten through twelfth grade. I am pleased to say that I did learn some things during that time; it wasn't a total waste of money while I figured out what I wanted to be when I grew up. The greatest lesson, though, was about the glory of God. I entered the Worship Leadership class in seminary one cold January morning expecting to learn about the practical aspects of planning church worship services and essentially to check that course off my list. What the professor actually did was spend that first week camped out in Isaiah 6; the Spirit of God helped us see first and foremost the one we were worshipping, Whom we would be helping others worship. Imagine that! Needing first to realize *whom* we worship before learning *how* to worship!

Isaiah needed that lesson, too. King Uzziah was dead. His 52-year reign brought stability, security, and prosperity. He mostly followed the Lord (2 Chr. 26). Now that he was dead, no one quite knew what would happen. At that precise moment in Isaiah's young life and in Israel's tumultuous history, God showed up. King Uzziah might have been dead, but Yahweh was not. The *whole* earth, marred though it was by human sin, was *still* full of his glory. God was still Holy, Sovereign, Merciful, and Indescribable. He was still doing his work in the world, working out a glorious plan of redemption. Isaiah would be the Lord's mouthpiece. That wasn't going to be an easy task, mostly because very few people were going to listen, but the awareness of God would sustain the prophet.

We, too, are called to speak the Word of God into our academic surroundings. Professors may have a powerful influence over the lives of young adults at a pivotal—even vulnerable—time in their lives. We can influence their career paths, their reading habits, their political activities, as well as their spiritual lives. Whatever else we might give them, the Word of God is the only thing that can provide our students with abundant life. That opportunity and obligation doesn't come without challenges: our profession is notoriously hostile to religion, and many of us would find it easier to keep our faith tucked away in our private lives. Like Isaiah, we must be aware of who God is; otherwise, we miss opportunities out of fear or laziness. Yahweh is still not dead. He is *still* doing his work in the world, working out a glorious plan of redemption. And he *still* chooses to use us to do it!

The Lord orchestrated my career path into archival work, but I have had the chance to teach classes on campus from time to time. I certainly could've been more *vocal* about my faith in the classroom. What I tried to *do*, however, was listen to my students, help them as much as possible, give them grace in their difficult times, and try to reduce their fear in speaking their opinions on difficult topics. Rarely did anyone turn down my offer to pray with them. Indeed, the most meaningful interactions of all were being able to pray with my students who were facing financial crises, the messy divorces of their parents, or hard decisions about their future. I hope and pray that they saw at least some of the glory of God in their interactions with me.

You and I may not have seen a literal vision of God like Isaiah did. Nonetheless, if we have repented and trusted in Jesus, we *have* seen God's glory (John 1:12). If they will do the same, our colleagues and students can also see God's glory. We of unclean lips in the midst of a people of unclean lips can have our guilt atoned for and allow his glory to shine through us to our students and colleagues.

— **Daniel Williams**, Integrative Studies,
Mercer University

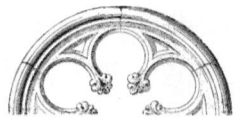

37

Sneakin' in Some Sacrifice and Sacrament

"Take, eat; this is My body. . . . Drink from it, all of you; for this is My blood of the covenant, which is being poured out for many for forgiveness of sins."

Matthew 26:26–28, NSAB

In the first part of my Moral Philosophy course, I used to show my students how Aristotle's teleological ethics begins with the simple truth that all human beings act for an end, and although some ends serve as means to higher ends, there is one ultimate end that everyone desires: happiness. But caution: Aristotle's meaning of happiness, *eudaimonia*, is best translated as human flourishing ("a good *life*" or "*being* good"), and this meaning should never be confused with today's prevailing idea that happiness is pleasure, "a good *time*" or "*feeling* good." When we look closely, a good life is one that acquires all the real goods that human beings need, obtained over a lifetime. Some of these real goods are limited (too much is not good for us) because they satisfy our lower bodily needs or give us physical pleasures, while others of these real goods are unlimited (one can never have too much) because they satisfy our higher, intellectual/spiritual needs or give us pleasures of the soul.

The highest of these real goods is Leisure, not in the modern sense of "lounging around" but in the intellectual/spiritual sense that includes the activities of learning, appreciating, and contemplating. Since Aristotle said that humans work in order to enjoy a life of Leisure (and not the other way around), I used this insight to get my students thinking about their future employment, especially when a really good life (Leisure) includes a meaningful spiritual life too.

In order to develop the idea of a meaningful spiritual life, I used Josef Pieper's idea that at the heart of true Leisure is *celebration*, not in the modern sense of "a party," but in the traditional sense where authentic celebration is ultimately rooted in *worship* . . . as in "celebrating" mass.[28] Pieper also said that true worship has two essential elements: sacrifice and sacrament.[29] To develop these concepts, I would show my students that worship practices found in the Old and New Testaments all included a sacrificial offering to God. In Genesis 22:1–14, Abraham builds an altar upon which to sacrifice his son, Isaac (although God replaces Isaac with a *ram*); in Matthew 26:26–28, (see also 1 Cor. 11:23–25), Jesus himself, the Son of God, becomes a sacrificial "*Lamb* of God" offering himself on the cross.

The ancient Hebrew celebrations reaffirmed their covenant with God as they sacrificed a goat or lamb on an altar in order to praise and thank him. Then, as his way of showing approval with this sacrifice, God gave this sacrificed animal back to his people to eat, to be nourished, and to make merry. Similarly, in the New Testament, Jesus established a new covenant when he broke bread at the Last Supper, commanding his followers to eat his body and drink his blood in remembrance of him

(Luke 22:14–20). And so, today, each time a priest consecrates the Eucharist on the altar, we celebrate this sacrament (i.e., an outward sign or symbol that is spiritually efficacious), as the consecrated bread and wine once again become Christ's body and blood that, as true spiritual food and drink, nourishes the human soul (John 6:51–58).

By sneakin' in this theological material into their philosophy class, I hoped to instill in my students a more expansive, spiritual understanding of Leisure, not just as some intellectual or aesthetic enrichment, but as that heavenly spring that alone quenches our spiritual thirst. Thus, Pieper shows that true Leisure includes a First Commandment-type selfless love for God and, when we love God above all else, this love cannot be given because of a received personal benefit; we either love God for who he is . . . or we do not love him at all.

Whether my students knew I was sneakin' in some theological insights about sacrifice and sacrament, I can't know for sure. And yet, there are two things that I do know for sure: first, as a professed Christian philosopher, my students shouldn't have expected anything less. And second, communicating these ultimate, spiritual truths was not only good for my students, it also was the right thing for me to do as well!

— **John G. Trapani Jr.**, Philosophy, Walsh University

145

38

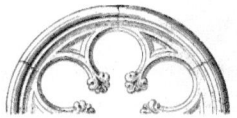

The Double Vocation

"For it is God which worketh in you both to will and to do of his good pleasure."

Philippians 2:13, KJV

"Answering the call of our Creator is 'the ultimate why' for living, the highest source of purpose in human existence. . . . Calling is the truth that God calls us to himself so decisively that everything we are, everything we do, and everything we have is invested with a special devotion and dynamism lived out as a response to his summons and service."[30]

Os Guinness

One summer in my teens, I had a literal mountaintop experience. At the Methodist youth camp in the north Georgia mountains, I felt the "call to preach." When I came home to my small town, I completed the process of acquiring the Methodist local license to preach, and I eventually was awarded a Christian Vocations scholarship at Duke University. I believed I was on my way to seminary and the pastoral ministry.

During my undergraduate years, however, I was "seduced"

by the French language. In the second semester of Wallace Fowlie's survey of French literature course, his lecture on a symbolist poem by Mallarmé was a veritable epiphany. As Fowlie, a master lecturer, guided us through that densely woven web of words, the poem seemed to open up to me like a beautiful flower. At that moment I somehow knew that making a poem come alive for students that way was what I most aspired to do in life.

I dedicated myself to studying the language, literature, and culture of France as my adopted profession, rather than the ministry. When I gave up my Christian Vocations scholarship, my advisor said I might still eventually become a lay preacher, but I did not really take that notion very seriously.

As director of a Center for Faith, Learning, and Vocation in the last two decades of my teaching career, my research on vocation led me to reflect on my faith journey and how God had led me to the work he had appointed me to accomplish in life. I began to understand that both the mountaintop call to preach and the love for French were paired experiences of God's call on my life.

Frederick Buechner once defined vocation as "the place where your deep gladness meets the world's deep need."[31] That means vocational discernment involves considering the particular gifts and strengths with which the Lord has endowed us. My deep joy came from French because God had given me an innate facility with language. I have always loved words. As a teaching scholar I was able to share that deep joy and a useful skill with young people. Moreover, I was able to share, both with students and with readers of my books, the wisdom of the great French religious writers. Finally, as a translator, I was able to make some of those writers' books available to people who could not read them in the original.

When God met me in the most personal way at age 30, I joined the Lay Witness Movement, and ever since then I have had occasional opportunities to preach in American churches, as well as on short-term mission trips abroad. To my surprise, my Christian Vocations advisor proved prophetic!

We are all called to live our lives in grateful response to God's saving grace: "Work willingly at whatever you do, as though you were working for the Lord rather than for people" (Col. 3:23, NLT). All of us are also called to "let the redeemed of the Lord say so" (Psalm 107:2, KJV). The ordained ministry is obviously not for everyone. But the priesthood of all believers entails carrying our faith into the workplace. My profession is that of teaching scholar, but my sacred responsibility is, in the words attributed to Saint Francis of Assisi, to "preach the gospel at all times and when necessary use words."[32]

— **John Marson Dunaway**, French and
Interdisciplinary Studies, Mercer University

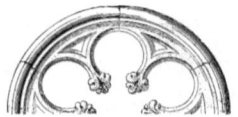

39

Moral Culpability and God's Omniscience

> "'Woman, where are they? Did no one condemn you?'
> And Jesus hastily adds: 'I do not condemn you, either.
> Go. From now on do not sin any longer.'"
>
> John 8:10–11, NASB

He cheated!
I knew him personally, not just as a student in my class . . . and he cheated! I even knew his family fairly well and still, he cheated!

My policy on cheating was very simple, mind you: if I catch you cheating on an exam, I will take your paper and walk you to the hallway; I will shake your hand and I will wish you well . . . and I will give you an F grade in the course.

This policy was unambiguous and amply promulgated. Since the stakes were high, generally the only ones who cheated were those who were not doing well and considered the gamble worth the risk. But Jim? He was an A student . . . and yet he cheated anyway! Our moment in the hallway was awkward. As I shook his hand, I could see tears welling up in his eyes even as, in his shame, he avoided looking at me. I understood that the reason he did what he did was to impress me, and getting caught only heightened his shame. And so, I wished him well and I meant it.

The theoretical backstory behind my policy was philosophically based and scripturally reinforced. First, there was the philosophical distinction between "Judgments about Actions" (where one makes a rational judgment that an action, like cheating, is an objectively morally unacceptable behavior) and "Judgments about Culpability" (where, in a specific case, one makes a judgment about a person's moral culpability). This latter judgment involves three criteria, the first is objective, while the second and third rely on God's omniscience . . . or not.

The first criterion requires that the action must really be objectively wrong; these are the philosophical judgments about actions *universally considered*. The second and third criteria require that the person committing the morally unacceptable action must *know* that the action is wrong, and must *freely* will it. The difficulty here is that, since no one person can ever know what another person knows, nor whether another person's choices are truly free, these last two criteria allow for two possibilities: *if* no omniscient power exists, then there is no real justice, only good or bad luck. On the other hand, *if* an omniscient God really does exist, then ultimately, there is true moral justice. Since an omniscient God knows each person better than that person knows him- or herself, God alone knows what we truly know, and he alone also would know the full measure of our freedom, weighing our choices against our all-too-human compulsions, habits, personal dispositions, and the like.

For me, this philosophical distinction is reinforced scripturally when Jesus judges the woman caught in adultery (John

8:1–11). After disarming the crowd ("Let him who is without sin cast the first stone," John 8:7, KJV), Jesus reveals his divine omniscience as he tenderly pardons her sin (the objectively immoral action of adultery), and, knowing her true innate goodness, he absolves her moral culpability as well.

As for Jim, having studied these things in the very Moral Philosophy class in which he cheated (ironic, right?!), he also knew intuitively that I held him in genuine esteem and affection no matter what he may have done, and, to his great credit and as a sign of his integrity, he enrolled in my course again the next semester . . . acing it entirely on his own abilities. Lesson learned.

We often hear the expression, "judge the sin, not the sinner." That is, while rationally we can discern objective moral wrongdoing, only God has the omniscience needed for a judgment of true moral culpability, especially since it was Jesus who came to heal sinners; "it is the sick who need the doctor" (Matt. 9:12). Perhaps French Catholic novelist, Léon Bloy, best captured the implications of this distinction when he penned these often-misunderstood lines: "There are no sinners in hell; sinners were the friends of Jesus. There are only the wicked."[33]

— **John G. Trapani Jr.**, Philosophy, Walsh University

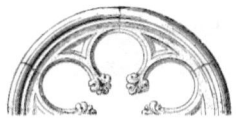

40

A Prayer for Writers

"Therefore I, the prisoner of the Lord, urge you to walk in a manner worthy of the calling with which you have been called."

Ephesians 4:1, NASB

There is little that is more central to all Abrahamic faiths than the written word. In fact, it is impossible to even imagine what our religion would be without writing. All religions have their texts, but few, if any, can describe themselves, as we do, as people of the book. This is perhaps an odd thing for Christians, given that Christ's only writing was done in sand and the words he wrote were never recorded. It is also odd because written words are so unstable, so unavoidably ambiguous, so easily corrupted by those who wish to use them for their own purposes, so given to disingenuousness. They retain their fluid meaning over time only when they are protected within the traditions of language practices we hardly even notice. There are practices—my own in law for example—in which preservation of a register of language so that our fluid words may evolve is thought to be a central function of the practice, but, for the most part, this is not true for other practices, including, as here, the practice of academic scholarship.

It is in this light that the following prayer for academic writers is offered as a devotion. I did not pray this prayer in my own practice. It is, instead, the product of having thought about a particular language practice for many years. I wish now that I had prayed it or something like it as I was writing as a constant reminder to think of all writing as if it were scriptural, and to my obligation toward the written words I used: a reflection of language as God's gift.

May my written words be truthful, for the words of my language are not my own but God's gracious gift to use for his purposes.

May I never use words as if they were my own, for each is "the choicest of relics."[34]

May each word come to me from its own region and each word seek its own companions. And may each tell all that it knows.

May I always know that the language I use, like everything else about me, reflects my fallen nature, for what speech was created for is praise and confession.

May I always know then that my use of language, as I write for my vocation, is always for the "lesser things" because there are goods, like justice and truth, to be found there.

May I always know as well that in these uses my words are incapable of capturing in their descriptions the truth of God's creation, incapable, that is, of any true description, including any true descriptions of that which is in my own heart. And may this chastise me.

May I always know not to complain in this, to have no

yearning for a world in which we are not fallen. For it simply is God's wish that it be so for us.

May I know that all God has created is good and, therefore, the divisions among us in our "battles of words" do not reflect a mythology of a creation in violence that must be fought or controlled, but are instead, in the musical analogy through which St. Augustine understood the City of God, rendered harmonious in the truthful mythology of a creation in peace.

May I know, then, that what is central to the goodness of the social conversations in which I write is that I accept our harmonious differences as just that, ask that all voices, all words, be heard so that the music is complete, and may I join in the playing of this music for the glory of God and not my own.

Dear Father, teach me then to write so that language is rescued from those who would corrupt it for their own purposes.

Dear Father, teach me then to write so that every mark may bear its brunt as in poetry or scripture.

Dear Father, teach me then to "walk worthy of the vocation wherein [I] am called" (Eph. 4:1).

Dear Father, teach me to write.

— **Jack L. Sammons**, Law, Mercer University

41

The Saving Power of
the Holy Face

"Jesus, remember me when You come into Your Kingdom."
Luke 23:42, NASB

There's a praise song that begins: "You sat down at the right hand of the Father in majesty."[35] As I sang that the other day, I found myself picturing the scene on Golgotha with the two thieves hanging on either side of Jesus's cross. Luke's account doesn't tell us which side the repentant thief is on, but great artists normally put him on Christ's right side. In western culture, that is the more favored side, at least partly because of Matthew 25:33, where Jesus is described at the Last Judgment inviting the sheep, the saved on his right hand, to enter heaven, while relegating the goats or the damned on his left hand to hell. The Latin word for left is *sinistra*, which is the root for our English word sinister. All this has led to a prejudice historically in our culture against left-handed people. *Dextra* is the Latin for right, which can also mean correct or straight or even upright, morally worthy.

When we look at Titian's late Renaissance (c. 1566) painting

"Christ and the Good Thief," for example, we as the spectators see the good thief on *our left*, but we need to be reminded that from Jesus's perspective, he's on *his right* hand.[36] Most of the eyewitnesses to the crucifixion probably viewed the good thief as condemned. The world saw the thief as damned, unworthy, despicable. But Jesus saw his repentant heart.

Lord, give us the eyes of Jesus as we look at the faces in our classrooms, especially those the world might condemn or whom we ourselves might judge harshly.

I find it intriguing that Titian's painting depicts the good thief as more vigorous than the sagging figure of the Savior next to him. Perhaps it's because the artist has chosen the moment after this man's pardon, for Christ has already died. The good thief may still be alive physically, but more importantly, his posture reflects his redeemed state. He is already entering into new life because, despite the jeers and taunts of the crowd, the penitent thief has been born again! His gaze is directed above toward heaven. He raises his right hand in praise, and his face wears an expression of one coming out of pain and anxiety into wonder.

A final note: We, like the thief, can live into the powerful promise of Galatians 2:20 because we, like him, have been crucified with Christ! The life we now live in the flesh we live by faith in the Son of God, who loved us and gave himself for us. And as John 8:35 declares, "If the Son therefore shall make you free, ye shall be free indeed" (KJV).

Postscript: The good thief, or Saint Dismas in the Catholic Church, is also known as a saint of the Holy Face, because although he, too, was suffering on a cross, he acknowledged his own guilt and publicly defended Jesus, rebuking the thief who had blasphemed him. Although the good thief saw the suffering, humiliated, and disfigured Face of Jesus, he recognized him as King. "'Jesus, remember me when You come into Your Kingdom'" (Luke 23:42, NIV). For this reason, I prefer to call him The Penitent Thief. Because Saint Dismas saw divinity in Christ's face, he received salvation. Catholics also preserve a tradition of "Devotion to the Holy Face" inspired by Saint Dismas. Certain devotees of the Holy Face have even said that contemplating the face of Jesus has the power to bring about the salvation of others.

— **John Marson Dunaway**, French and
   Interdisciplinary Studies, Mercer University

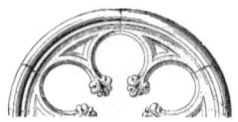

42

Meditation on Mercy

"I love the Lord, because he hath heard my voice and my supplications. Because he hath inclined his ear unto me, therefore will I call upon him as long as I live. The sorrows of death compassed me, and the pains of hell gat hold upon me: I found trouble and sorrow. Then called I upon the name of the Lord; O Lord, I beseech thee, deliver my soul. Gracious is the Lord, and righteous; yea, our God is merciful."

Psalm 116:1–5, KJV

*M*ercy. A beautiful word. A priceless gift when given and received as the Psalmist attests in Psalm 116. Found in many languages, the word for *mercy* in Hebrew is *hesed* (lovingkindness), in Aramaic *raham* (showing tender affection or compassion), and the Etruscan *merc* means exchange: value given and received between people.

Mercy is God's language of abiding relationship with creation and humanity. Day and night, season following season, creation offers us abundant gifts of mercy. They flow as water around boulders, drop as nourishing rain on parched ground, draw fresh growth from winter slumber, produce nourishing harvest, and sustain our lives through the exchange of the life-giving breath of the universe.

God's most profound gift of mercy is love embodied in Jesus Christ. In relinquishing power and control for love, God grants human beings freedom and simultaneously invites us into intimate relationship. Jesus conveys the reciprocal quality of mercy when he says, "Blessed are the merciful, for they shall receive mercy" (Matt. 5:7, ESV). In his life and his death, Jesus reveals the character of mercy.

In *The Merchant of Venice*, Shakespeare reflects on the human value of mercy: "The quality of mercy is not strained / It droppeth as the gentle rain / Upon the place beneath; it is twice blessed; / It blesseth him who gives and him who takes."[37]

Experiencing God's boundless mercy, we understand that human mercy dare never be contrived. Offered unconditionally, absent of judgment, seeing beyond illusions and beneath the surfaces of fear, mercy forgives and frees from all faults through courtesy, compassion, and grace. Mercy provides the humus of peace and justice. Relinquishing self-sufficiency and emptying ourselves of our own importance, we prepare our souls for the exchange of the priceless twice-blessed gifts of mercy.

Each morning in study or in classroom, we prepare to receive and to give the merciful exchange designed in the cosmos.

— **Ruthann Knechel Johansen**,
   Professor Emerita, University of Notre Dame,
   President Emerita, Bethany Theological Seminary

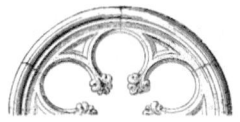

43

What Is Truth?

"Ye shall know the Truth, and the Truth shall set you free."
John 8:32, KJV

J ohn the Apostle's line can be found over the portal of many a university entrance gate. I thus have ever been mindful of the real connection that can exist between the true and the good, and between philosophical truth and becoming open to the reality of God: a life-goal that is absolutely good and that may await us in a life that will never end, should we come to use our freedom as it was originally intended to be used: to love and pursue what is truly good.

I have taught undergraduate students for 40 years at the University of San Francisco. They came from two significantly different groups. Roughly the first half of my teaching was to students in a Catholic Great Books program. It was composed of three sub-groups: intellectually minded Catholic students thirsting to understand better their own spiritual and intellectual tradition; non-Catholics likewise thirsting for intellectual truth and drawn to the program by the works to be encountered in it; and Catholic students enrolled in the program probably through their parents' insistence. The latter always posed the most difficult problem for the professors in the program, but the other two groups led to many dazzling and spirit-filled conversations. One could sense the deepening of life and an orientation to the true, the good, and the beautiful that was at work in the souls of the students.

The program's purpose was to prepare students for life in a pluralistic, increasingly secular world, one that could be hostile to the tradition they were "soaking up." I taught them for that reason, that was the *telos* of all that went on in the classroom, this "opening up" of their spirit to a greater world, one that is the true home of the human spirit at its best. It was a remarkable, Spirit-filled program, and its courses were ever a delight for me to teach.

In the other courses I taught outside Great Books, the students were quite different. An eclectic group from the student body at large, most were uninterested in my philosophy course (which they took only to fulfill a university requirement) and most brought to the class a mind formed chiefly by a secular truth inimical to spiritual reality. For this group, I emphasize what I take to be an almost unarguable truth: a university is a place dedicated primarily to the true. It is not aimed first at directing the will or furthering whatever "social project" of "liberation" might be dear to them. No: it is aimed at "knowing what is the case." I engage them the way Socrates did, not revealing my own mind, but encouraging them to grapple with what they themselves really know and hold. For, contrary to a glib relativism, they do not think slavery or genocide can be OK in some "possible world," but instead they are committed within to certain truths. Neither do they think that, if they open up their craniums, they will discover the idea of beauty or the

love they bear each other (when they do), but only a fantasti-
cally complicated electro-chemical "gray matter." We read the
texts, try to understand what they say: what is the case in them,
what their arguments are. Yet I engage with them in this work
with the hope that, indirectly and behind what we do, they will
be enabled to detect a larger "field of life" in which to move.
The work with them is much more difficult, the "new life" discovered apparently far less in evidence than it was in that first
group of students; but the ultimate goal remains the same and
my own sense of being of some worth to students comes from
those "inner connections" I can see being made.

"A mind is a terrible thing to waste" and a heart's loss even
more terrible.[38] And I hope I manage to make it plain to as many
as possible that, behind and in everything we do, it is their mind
and heart that is at stake, and that each of them possesses something deeply precious, to be nurtured and not lost.

— **Michael D. Torre**, Philosophy,
   University of San Francisco

44

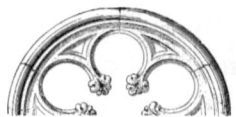

The Seat of the Scornful

One day as I was reading the beginning of a book titled *Through the Psalms with Derek Prince*, I was struck with his meditation on Psalm 1:1–3, a passage that I had memorized many years before.

> Blessed are those that walk not in the counsel of
>   the ungodly,
> nor stand in the way of sinners,
> nor sit in the seat of the scornful.
> But their delight is in the law of the Lord,
> and in His law do they meditate day and night.
> And they shall be like trees planted by the rivers of water
> that bring forth their fruit in their season.
> Their leaf also shall not wither,
> and whatsoever they do shall prosper.[39]

Those three verses have richly nourished me over the years. At an earlier time, I had heard a teaching on the importance of meditating on scripture. Memorizing any poem enables us to make it our own. If we memorize a passage like this one and chew or ruminate on it day and night—sort of like a cow chewing cud—the inimitable power of God's word is released in us. Dwelling on the word throughout the day begins to show us truths we didn't detect from simply reading through the words. We allow room in our heart for the Holy Spirit to communicate with our spirit in a fruitful collaboration.

I recall an occasion when I was prompted to carry out one of the specific applications of this passage. That occasion was during the tumultuous days decades ago when our faculty was bitterly divided over what many saw as the administration's top-down management and profligate spending. The faculty lunch table in the snack bar became an extended gripe session of cynical criticism. All the negativity was eroding my joy and peace.

When I was appointed co-chair of the watchdog committee charged with investigating the alleged administrative abuses, it proved to be one of the most brutally painful times of my life. With chairing the department, plus the campus-wide contentiousness, my time and energy were being consumed by administrative duties that were robbing me of the more fulfilling work of teaching and writing. Our committee members were labeled as ungrateful malcontents, and one trustee even published a letter advising us to "love the university or leave it." I remember realizing I was "sitting in the seat of the scornful."

I knew I needed to find a more peaceful place for lunch, so I started having a light lunch in the office and then going out to the park adjacent to campus and lying on the grass, praying and meditating in silence. I allowed the tranquility of the place to calm my spirit.

As I look back, I firmly believe God blessed me in just the way David describes in verse three. I now indeed feel very much "like a tree planted by the rivers of water." My life is certainly not free of problems, but my children, their spouses, and my grandchildren are the flourishing leaves that have not withered. And I myself have flourished beyond what I could have dreamed. My involvement in interdisciplinary courses helped enrich my classroom experience and my development as a teacher, and it provided a wider circle of relationships with both colleagues and students. I helped start a Faculty/Staff Christian Fellowship on campus. And through a Lilly grant I was blessed with opportunities to strengthen the religious heritage of my university as well as networking with Christian colleagues all over the country.

The stage of my career since the campus political crisis proved to be the most rewarding years of my tenure as a faculty member. Eventually, after the crisis between faculty and administration ended, I was grateful to be able to return to the faculty lunch table and again enjoy the fellowship of my colleagues.

— **John Marson Dunaway**, French and
  Interdisciplinary Studies, Mercer University

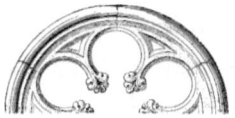

45

Enough

"It is not that we think we are qualified to do anything on our own. Our qualification comes from God."

2 Corinthians 3:4–6, NLT

"Each time he said, 'My grace is all you need. My power works best in weakness.'"

2 Corinthians 12:9, NLT

Those of us who have spent any time in academia know the definition of rubric. We create rubrics, we grade with them, we ourselves are even assessed by them, whether it is for a grant submission, manuscript, or promotion and tenure package. Sometimes the rubrics are clear and straightforward, other times they may be vague, and sometimes we aren't quite sure what we are being measured against. This constant questioning of "Am I doing enough?" begins during our experience as doctoral students receiving critiques from advisors and committee members, looking for that stamp of approval with every draft until we defend. For me, I realized that as an academician my brain was trained to constantly assess, compare, evaluate all my actions against a real or assumed rubric of "enough." Am I good enough? Am I working enough? Am I enough for this rigorous workplace?

As someone with a goal-oriented personality and high standards for myself (with which I can assume many of you in the Academy reading this can identify), I am immensely grateful for my faith—my belief in God and identity in Christ—that provides a rubric outside of my work. That there is another metric to be evaluated by, not by my contributions, but rather by my position in Christ. I think often about what Paul writes in Second Corinthians: our adequacy coming from God and our sufficiency not coming from ourselves. When we think deeper about this concept, it is close to the exact opposite of what we are conditioned to believe by the Academy. From the academic viewpoint we are taught that our worth and contribution and legacy are measured by the number of papers or books published, grants submitted, classes taught, or committees on which we've served. From the biblical perspective we know that our worth is based on nothing of our own doing. Intertwining these two very different perspectives can feel challenging, especially for a new academic, to decide which rubric to prioritize.

For me it is a constant values challenge to remember where my worth is found, and at the same time it has provided me immense freedom. I can be a productive member of my university and strive for excellence in teaching—hypothetically being 'enough' based on the rubrics of my supervisors—and still fall short. I had this happen recently when I was praised in my annual review for all I was accomplishing. But then it was misconstrued by another supervisor as an issue with my time management skills that I could not do all that was assigned to me. My first reaction was to get upset and to try and prove that

I was more than good enough, that I was doing enough to shout my worth. After some time and clarification, I realized that the issue was rooted in miscommunication, and it had nothing to do with my performance or capability. The stress and frustration I felt were not exactly about that moment, there are harder challenges yes, but it reminded me of how that "good enough" conditioning that we have experienced can make us sensitive to being judged. I needed the reminder I am writing about now— that I am enough in Christ no matter what I produce.

May we all be fruitful members of the Academy, knowing that our rubric is different and that in Christ we are always enough.

— **Lauren E. Futrell Dunaway**, Public Health,
    Tulane University

46

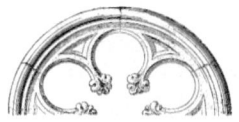

The Shared Life

"We proclaim to you the One who existed from the
beginning, whom we have heard and seen. We saw Him
with our own eyes and touched Him with our own hands."

1 John 1:1, NLT

"Of His fulness have all we received."

John 1:16, KJV

I n 2018, a dear colleague and I accompanied a group of nine
students on a three-week visit to N'Zérékoré in the West African country of Guinea. This unforgettable experience, which
included a week's prior preparation as well as a final week of
debriefing on campus, was part of a program that my university
calls Mercer on Mission (MOM). Designed as a service-learning course immersing us in the culture of a developing country, it is a signature program of Mercer. We had led a group
to Senegal a few years previously to work with the farmers in
the Senegal River Delta. In both MOM trips, we studied West
African literature, history, and culture in two courses that my
colleague and I offered. But much of our time was spent living

with our students and working with the Senegalese farmers or tutoring the Guinean children at Home of Hope, an orphanage founded by our former student, Samuel Johnson. We learned to eat with our fingers from a common bowl and drink hot mint tea in the cool shade, even sweeter than the iced tea back home in Georgia! This intimate level of relationship made life-long friends of all the participants. Some of the students even joined me for morning devotionals. Transformational learning has been a hallmark of the Mercer curriculum from the time I arrived fresh out of graduate school in 1972.

Spending time with students outside the classroom is an excellent opportunity to have a lasting redemptive impact on their lives. After all, God calls us to be teachers for his own purposes, which include both helping form young lives for him and being formed by them.

Not all universities have a program like Mercer on Mission, but all Christian professors can make opportunities outside the classroom to get to know their students as whole human beings rather than entries in the roll book. I also have fond memories of taking students on field trips to a monastery or a museum or inviting them over for a home-cooked meal.

The great Dietrich Bonhoeffer wrote a wonderful book called *Life Together*. It grew out of the experience of establishing an underground seminary, in protest of the official German church's collaboration with the Nazis. He lived with the seminarians in a communal setting, as well as teaching them. His constant presence amounted to what is now called "incarnational ministry," which entails moving into the oppressed community so as to minister holistically in a shared life.

Our Lord Jesus, who was the Master Teacher, invited his students to live with him, travel with him, share meals with him.

One of the reasons they were able to perpetuate his memory is that, according to John, they had an intimately close relationship with him in "the shared life" of the twelve.

We don't all have to go to West Africa, but we can all ask the Lord how he would like us to share life with our students.

— **John Marson Dunaway**, French and
  Interdisciplinary Studies, Mercer University

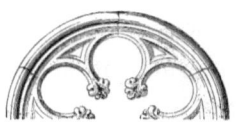

47

Divine Self-disclosure:
A Meditation on the Nature of God

"How great a forest is set ablaze by a small fire!"

James 3:5, NAS

Professors live in a world of words. We are paid, quite literally, to think and then to talk about what we have been contemplating. But "How great a forest is set ablaze by a small fire!" (Jas. 3:5, NAS) is what St. James says about our speech. The Scriptures are full of warnings about keeping watch over our words, and those warnings apply at least as much to our teaching and research as they do to our office banter and mentoring. We seldom pause to wonder why such an emphasis appears so often. But the insistence that every word be measured is far more than just practical; it is part of our mystical life in Christ.

Aristotle believed in a God who could not communicate with humanity. The reasoning was simple: God was the perfect being, and since we become what we contemplate, if God looked at something like us—imperfect—he would bring that contemplated imperfection into himself, and he would be unmade: Perfect Being cannot contemplate anything, Aristotle said, but itself.

But Christian faith forwarded a different, more vibrant view. God was not just the perfection of being, but the *loving* perfection of being. And you cannot keep love to yourself. God, thus, in his own eternal and perfect being, engages in an act of *self-disclosure*. He speaks of himself. And this is where it gets interesting.

Since God is *absolutely complete and perfect* Being, the Word he speaks to disclose himself is, necessarily, *absolutely complete and perfect*. This act of self-disclosure is so perfect, in fact, that it communicates (more than that: it *is*) his very Being, itself. The Word spoken is the same Being as the Father who speaks. And this self-disclosure is so complete and full and vibrant that, just as the Father lives, the disclosure is itself a living expression of the very essence of the Father: it is a living person. And yet, this self-disclosure is separate from the Father (otherwise, it could not be *self-disclosure*, but only self-awareness). The Son is God, just as the Father is God. But the Son is not the Father.

And since there are now two persons, communion is possible. The Father and the Son can commune with one another because they are different persons. But since they are one Being, their communion is an absolute and perfected communion between the two absolute and perfect persons in one Being: the Father and the Son. And this communion between the Father and the Son is the very love that is the Being of God. The Father and the Son love one another with a perfection of love that is so vibrant and full and living that it is itself a third living person—and of course, this person, too, being a perfect expression of the perfect love that is God, is himself the same Being who is the Father and the Son. Christians know this person as the Holy Spirit.

When St. Peter tells the exiled churches: "He that would love life and see good days, let him keep his tongue from evil and his lips from speaking guile" (1 Pet. 3:10, NLT) his advice—almost certainly he is quoting an ancient hymn—is far more than pragmatic baseline life-coaching. He is being a mystic. He is reminding us that every act of *speaking* is a primary jewel in our ability to bear the image of God. And communication is a formidable responsibility, precisely because it imitates the very Being of God himself, wrapped in the mystery of his own self-disclosure.

Every time we open our mouth, wheels of fire spin within wheels of fire. We—like God—disclose ourselves. And our revelation is, all too often, not particularly flattering. We set out to teach what is true, and yet if we are honest, we find that all too often we end up trying to impress others and show how smart we are, instead. May the Almighty God, Father, Son, and Holy Spirit, help us all "keep watch at the door of our lips" (Ps. 141:3, Gelineau translation).

— Mark A. E. Williams,
California State University, Sacramento

48

Finding Rest in God in the Information Age

> "Woe to me! . . . I am worn out with groaning and find no rest."
>
> Jeremiah 45:3, NIV

I
n today's digital culture, a person can literally be busy 24/7. We have more information available to us than ever before in history. We can find anything with an internet search. As professors, we all know the feeling of information overload. So much to read, so much to consider, and so much to think about.

Throughout the Bible, writers talk about the importance of rest. Some writers lament that they have no rest. Job said, "I have no rest, but only turmoil" (Job 3:26, NIV). The psalmist wrote, "My God, I cry out by day, but you do not answer, by night, but I find no rest" (Ps. 22:2, NIV). And Jeremiah wrote, "Woe to me! I am worn out with groaning and find no rest" (Jer. 45:3, NIV).

The word *rest* in the Bible is used in many ways. The first way we find it used is by God himself. In Genesis, the Bible says that after God finished his work, he rested on the seventh day. Even

God knew the importance of resting. And he modelled it for us. He then instructed us to take a sabbath day of rest. Lest we think that the sabbath is just for Old Testament believers, the New Testament writer in the book of Hebrews says that "There remains, then, a Sabbath-rest for the people of God" (Heb. 4:9, NIV).

Professors sometimes find it hard to take a day of rest. I know that is true for me. There are always more papers to grade and more articles to write. But somehow when I take time to rest and get refreshed, God multiplies the time during the other six days.

Another way the Bible uses the word rest is in the sense of finding our rest in God. As David writes in the Psalms, "Truly my soul finds rest in God; my salvation comes from him" (Ps. 62:1, NIV). I believe that as human beings we long for a rest of peace in our innermost beings. This is a rest that is free from anger, free from agitation, free from turmoil, and free from the devastating consequences of living in a fallen world.

But where can we find such a rest? David writes that it can be found in God alone. He is our source of rest, of peace, and well-being. By taking time daily in God's Word to meditate on his truth, we can find rest for our souls. With Christ, we can pour out our deepest longings to him knowing that he hears and answers us when we come to him.

At Western Washington University where I teach, I try to join with other professors and staff each week for a time of prayer. During COVID-19 we met to pray on Zoom. It was a wonderful time to join with other Christ followers, to come before the Lord with our needs, and to place our trust in him. In him we can find rest for our souls.

A third sense of the word rest in the Bible is used in Isaiah where the writer says, "The Spirit of the LORD will rest on him—the Spirit of wisdom and of understanding, the Spirit of counsel and of might, the Spirit of knowledge and fear of the Lord" (Isa. 11:2, NIV). Not only can we take a day of rest, find our rest in the Lord, but the Lord's Spirit can rest or reside on us. And his Spirit can give us all that we need as professors— wisdom, understanding, counsel, knowledge, and the fear of the Lord.

May we as Christian professors allow the Holy Spirit to rest on our lives so that we can be light in our world.

— **Geri Forsberg**, English,
Western Washington University

49

My Foolishness and
God's Wisdom

"Don't be too proud to enjoy the company of ordinary people. And don't think you know it all."

Romans 12:16, NLT

J. R. R. Tolkien never did systematic theology. But his literary opus, *The Lord of the Rings*, as well as the larger Middle Earth legendarium, is chock full of theological insights. Tolkien masterfully, and subtly, "does theology" through the words and deeds of his fictional characters.

Rereading the books, I was struck by words that Tolkien puts in the hobbit Merry Brandybuck's mouth in *The Return of the King*:

> It is best to love first what you are fitted to love, I suppose: you must start somewhere and have some roots, and the soil of the Shire is deep. Still there are things deeper and higher; and not a gaffer could tend his garden in what he calls peace but for them, whether he knows about them or not. I am glad that I know about them, a little.[40]

The first time I read *The Lord of the Rings* I was in high school. I'm sure the wisdom of this passage, and many others like it, didn't resonate so deeply as they do now. Time and experience have tilled the soil of my heart and mind such that Merry's words, as I read them today, are more deeply impressed.

What I take from Merry, and from Tolkien, is an uncommon humility. And with it, deep Christian wisdom.

As intellectuals, many of us fancy ourselves wise, and we're generally pleased with ourselves for it. After all, our knowledge is hard won and (hopefully) contributes something of value to our communities. But the danger of being learned is conflating knowledge with wisdom. Knowledgeable people are not always wise. And sometimes wise persons have very limited knowledge, in the word's narrowest sense.

As a hobbit who loves frequent meals, pipeweed, and a cozy armchair by the fire, Merry isn't naturally predisposed to seek out the high and lofty mysteries. He knows about them "a little," and is wise enough to realize they are important. He genuinely loves the things he is "fitted to love," but also recognizes that the simplicity and security of the Shire is only possible because "things deeper and higher" are there to ground, direct, and protect it.

Contrast Merry with the typical academic. In our educated hubris, we tend to judge the bourgeois masses for their simple pleasures. Perched atop self-aggrandizing castles, thinking persons can be smug in our dismissal of life's "lesser" pursuits, whether football or fashion. I'm too often party to such conceit.

Tolkien's wisdom in Merry shames me. The hobbit knows, as I also do but often forget, that in his merciful humility, God "fits" each soul according to his purposes, in due time. All loves, when properly ordered in Christ, serve to build up the believer in faith. It's true that many times our loves are disordered, and that football or fashion can become idols. But it's also true that love abides all things to transfigure them, and us, by the light of grace.

Who am I to judge God's temporal "fitting" of my neighbors' (or my students') loves, loves that God may be using for his eternal purposes? Where we think we see arrested development, God could be working out his plans, imperceivably, precisely through those things that—in our vain sophistication—we ignore or denigrate.

I think this is why Paul tells the Romans not to scorn the company of ordinary people. He's not being patronizing or suggesting that all loves, all tastes, all pursuits, are equal. Rather, it's a nod to the fact that God alone fits us to the life best suited for love to take root. As I would have it, when I'm frustrated or impatient, others would cast their "lesser" loves into the fire. In my pride, I would deign to limit the ways that God loves us, loves me, into being.

What a fool I can be.

— **A. Chase Mitchell**, Media and Communication,
East Tennessee State University

50

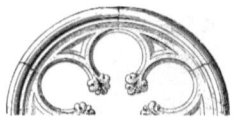

Clinging to the Rock

"There is no one holy like the Lord; there is no one besides you; there is no Rock like our God."

1 Samuel 2:2, NIV

When my son was little, I'd take him to the beach to hunt for pretty rocks. We looked for unique, shiny, beautiful ones. Sometimes we'd go to the local rock show where we could buy polished ones.

Rocks have always been fascinating to me. As a professor in the university, I think our students are also searching for rocks. They are searching for something unique, something solid, something that has substance. They want to find something that is real and true—something they can hold on to.

The Bible tells us that Jesus Christ is our Rock, and he is unique. "There is no one holy like the Lord; there is no one besides you; there is no Rock like our God" (1 Sam. 2:2, NIV). The Bible goes on to describe our God as a perfect Rock, a just Rock, a Rock who protects, a Rock who delivers, a Rock who redeems our lives, a Rock who saves. He is a Rock who is living. He is an eternal Rock. The writer of Isaiah says, "Trust in the

Lord forever, for the Lord, the Lord himself, is the Rock eternal" (Isa. 26:4, NIV).

God is an accessible Rock; we can speak to him, and he listens. The psalmist prayed to God saying, "To you, Lord, I call; you are my Rock, do not turn a deaf ear to me" (Ps. 28:1, NIV). Our God hears and listens to us. We can always go to him.

God is also a Rock who educates and trains us for the work we must do. David the psalmist wrote, "Praise be to the Lord my Rock, who trains my hands for war, my fingers for battle" (Ps. 144:1, NIV). God wants to be part of our educational process.

University students (and all of us) are immersed in disinformation, misinformation, fake news, media manipulation and propaganda. Social media have produced a type of sinking-sand environment. The Bible tells us not to build our lives on a foundation of sand, but on the living Rock.

The Bible also warns people not to forget the Rock. In Isaiah we read, "You have forgotten God your Savior; you have not remembered the Rock, your fortress" (Isa. 17:10, NIV). And the psalmist is encouraged that the people "remembered that God was their Rock, that God Most High was their Redeemer" (Ps. 78:35, NIV).

As Christians, we can point our students, co-workers, and neighbors to the eternal, living, saving, protecting Rock. We can help them search for the Rock that is beautiful. As a Christian professor, I can do that as I bring Christ into my research and publishing, and into my classroom discussions. Regardless of our vocation, we can point our students, co-workers, and neighbors toward the Rock as we take time to pray for and with them.

Several years ago, a former student returned to campus the night I was speaking to the Christian students. He came up to me after I finished speaking to tell me that because of my prayers with him in my office many years earlier, the direction of his life was completely changed. The student is following the leading of Jesus Christ. Our students are searching. Regardless of our position, we can help others find and hold on to the Rock.

— **Geri Forsberg**, English,
Western Washington University

51

The Work of (Y)our Hands

> "Yet you, Lord, are our Father. We are the clay, you are the potter; we are all the work of your hand."
>
> Isaiah 64:8, NIV

Growing up, my mom, Deborah Elizabeth Mitchell (née Vestal), would sometimes remind me that my fourth-great grandfather had been a prominent nineteenth-century potter. Born in 1828 in Washington County, Virginia, Jessee Vestal was part of the Great Road tradition, best known for his stoneware vessels. His masterpiece, which dates to 1849, is a large brandy jug. Its face bears his name and an original poem in incised script:

Long and lazy
little and loud
fair and foolish
dark and proud
a splendee branda jug[41]

Before I returned to academia as faculty, while I was completing my dissertation, I worked for William King Museum of Art in Abingdon, Virginia. On my first day, I was pleasantly surprised to learn that Jessee's "poem jug" was part of WKMA's Cultural Heritage Project. The piece had been found broken in pieces under the porch of a country house in Chilhowie, not far from Jessee's lifelong home in Alvarado—a small community on the South Fork of the Holston River. The shards were reassembled and, some years later, the restored piece is now on display in a permanent exhibit at the museum.

Jessee's craft and poem jug have provided spiritual sustenance to me, on several levels. It has also informed the ways I approach my vocation as a professor and scholar.

The name Vestal is of French (Huguenot) origin. An altered form of Vassal, it was a status name for medieval retainers. A vassal was a personal follower of a landowning lord. The vassal and his lands were subject to the sovereignty of the landholder, yet he was considered part of the lord's household. In Christ, as vassals of our Lord, we are members of his household; subject to his rule, yes, but willing followers, confidants, and brothers and sisters in arms—not of sword and shield, but of love.

Vestal/vassal also conjures the *vessel*. As dust-born creatures, God makes his home with us by pouring out his Spirit into these earthly bodies. The author of life chose Jesse of Bethlehem to establish the house of David, the conduit and vessel from whom Christ would come. But it took time, patience, and endurance for David's heir to be revealed in the flesh. Over centuries, through many turns of the Potter's wheel, Israel was being molded and reformed.

As educators, we can get caught up in seeing the fruits of our labor manifest in clear, concrete ways, and we want to know how our efforts are making a difference *now*. We write annual reports documenting our teaching, research, and service activities, with an emphasis on measurable impact. We obsess about the particularities of our research and hope large audiences attend our conference presentations. We wonder if and how our work benefits students in real and lasting ways, and we celebrate or lament course evals at the end of each term.

Yet the work of our hands—the spiritual fruits of our labor—will not be fully revealed until the end. Like Jessee Vestal, we have no way of knowing when or how our work will affect others. How could he have imagined his fourth-great grandson, in 2025, pecking out a devotional about him on a laptop (a what?)?

I look forward to discovering, in the fullness of time, what God has in store. I wait for the day when the work of my hands, as a teacher, mentor, and colleague, is made manifest through the work of his hands. Long and lazy, little and loud, fair and foolish, dark and proud, I may yet be, but in the end Christ's work in and through me is, I pray, quite splendee.

"And let the beauty of the Lord our God be upon us: and establish thou the work of our hands upon us; yea, the work of our hands establish thou it." (Psalm 90:17, KJV)[42]

— **A. Chase Mitchell**, Media and Communication, East Tennessee State University

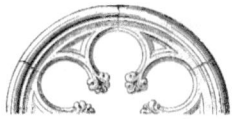

52

This is Big!

"God that made the world and all things therein . . . is Lord of heaven and earth. . . . For in him we live, and move, and have our being."

Acts 17:24a; 28a, KJV

Life in the modern Academy can feel constraining. We find ourselves hemmed in by departmental silos, disciplinary boundaries, and methodological gatekeepers. Academic publication often constricts us to an extremely specific research focus within a narrow subdiscipline. While specialization yields valuable depth, it can create a constricted vision in which we "miss the forest for the trees," or, in our case, the university for the lab or even the universe for the university.

For Christians in the Academy, the constraints may feel more pronounced. We might perceive a tension between academic pursuits and faith commitments, questioning whether certain research paths or conclusions are open to us. Perhaps we feel pressure to defend our faith or compartmentalize our faith. We worry about crossing boundaries imposed by academic cultures, disciplinary norms, or religious communities. The resulting intellectual claustrophobia can stifle both scholarly creativity and spiritual vitality.

Christian teaching offers a liberating corrective to this constrained vision. Jesus is not merely the greatest being among beings but Being itself—the very source and fulfillment of all being. Colossians 1:16–17 teaches, "all things have been created through him and for him. He is before all things, and in him all things hold together" (NASB). The modern conception of religion as an optional accessory of life cannot confine Jesus because he is Life itself.

Paul's sermon in Athens (Acts 17) speaks good news to modern Christian scholars as it did to ancient pagan scholars. Paul proclaimed that far from being confined to a religious compartment of life, God "is Lord of heaven and earth." All being is from and sustained in God.

This cosmic understanding transforms our academic vocation. As Creator, Sustainer, and Redeemer of all, Jesus is the source and fulfillment of all beauty, goodness, and truth in the universe and the university. There is no other source. When we truly grasp this claim, we are liberated to approach our academic work as an expression of our faith. Every field of study becomes ground where we encounter aspects of God's creation and truth.

As Paul reminded the Corinthians who had divided themselves among different teachers: "All things are yours, whether Paul or Apollos or Cephas or the world or life or death or the present or the future—all are yours, and you are of Christ, and Christ is of God" (1 Cor. 3:21–23, NIV). In Christ, the full spectrum of knowledge belongs to us.

As Christians, we are free to pursue truth with courage, curiosity, and joy. We need not be anxious about who discovers truth or how they discover it because all truth is from God. We need not fear where truth will lead because all truth leads ultimately to God. We can be confident that in studying any aspect of creation faithfully, we encounter traces of its Creator. We find freedom and joy in knowing that all genuine truth—whether discovered in a laboratory, library, or liturgy—ultimately begins and ends in God. All genuine truth belongs to Christ and, therefore, to us as his followers.

— **James W. Vining**, Communication Studies,
Governors State University

Notes

[1] Dedication. Genesis 2:18 says God gives Adam a "help meet," the King James language for a helper who is fitting, suitable.

[2] Acknowledgements. See Faculty Commons, https://www.cru.org/faculty/about/missional-moments/.

[3] Acknowledgements. See Campus Crusade for Christ, https://www.cru.org/.

[4] Introduction. Dennis F. Kinlaw, "May 26: Tabernacle in your Midst," in *This Day with the Master: 365 Daily Meditations* (Grand Rapids: Discovery House Publishers, 2002).

[5] Introduction. Geoffrey Chaucer, *The Canterbury Tales*, trans. Nevill Coghill (London: Penguin Classics, 2003), "The Clerk's Tale," line 310.

[6] Devotional 2, Blessings in the Challenge: Part 2. For clarification of faculty members' legal rights to express religious views in various settings, see Rick Hove and Heather Holleman, *A Grander Story: An Invitation to Christian Professors* (Orlando, FL: Cru Press, 2017) Appendices A and B, 197–211.

[7] Devotional 5, Redeeming the Time. Marcus Hummon et al., "Bless the Broken Road," performed by Rascal Flatts, *Feels Like Today*, Lyric Street Records, 2004, CD.

[8] Devotional 7, Our Work as Worship. Abraham Kuyper, "Sphere Sovereignty," in *Abraham Kuyper: A Centennial Reader*, ed. James D. Bratt (Grand Rapids: Eerdmans, 1998), 488.

[9] Devotional 9, A Peddler of Hope. Geoffrey Chaucer, *The Canterbury Tales*, General Prologue, lines 307–310 (Middle English: "And gladly wolde he lerne and gladly teche"), in *The Riverside Chaucer*, ed. Larry D. Benson (Boston: Houghton Mifflin, 1987), 287–310.

[10] Devotional 9, A Peddler of Hope. Frank Bruni, "How to Get the Most Out of College," *The New York Times*, August 17, 2018, https://www.nytimes.com/2018/08/17/opinion/college-students.html.

[11] Devotional 9, A Peddler of Hope. Fred Rogers, quoted in *Wisdom from the World According to Mister Rogers: Important Things to Remember* (New York: Peter Pauper Press, 2006), 93.

[12] Devotional 9, A Peddler of Hope. Parker J. Palmer, *Let Your Life Speak: Listening for the Voice of Vocation* (San Francisco: Jossey-Bass, 2000), Chapter 1.

[13] Devotional 11, A Physician Professor Who Could Not Heal Himself. Paul Tillich, "Religion and Secular Culture," in *The Theology of Culture*, ed. Robert C. Kimball (New York: Oxford University Press, 1959), 42. Note: the exact phrase used in the original is, "Religion is the substance of culture, and culture is the form of religion."

[14] Devotional 15, See How the Holy Spirit Works! Elizabeth Barrett Browning, "Aurora Leigh," in *The Poetical Works of Elizabeth Barrett Browning*, ed. Ruth M. Adams (New York: Houghton Mifflin, 1974), 372.

[15] Devotional 15, See How the Holy Spirit Works! See Walsh University, https://www.walsh.edu/index.html.

[16] Devotional 18, A Pearl of Great Price. Simone Weil, *Waiting for God*, trans. Emma Craufurd (New York: G. P. Putnam's Sons, 1951), 106.

[17] Devotional 25, The Devotional Life for Followers of Jesus. Joseph McRae Mellichamp, *Ministering in the Secular University: A Guide for Christian Professors and Staff* (St. Louis: Lewis and Stanley, 1997).

[18] Devotional 26, The Eyes of the Heart. Joyce Kilmer, "Trees," lines 11–12, in *Trees and Other Poems* (New York: George H. Doran Company, 1914), 19.

[19] Devotional 28, Summoned. Pablo Neruda, "Poetry," lines 1–2, in *The Essential Neruda: Selected Poems*, ed. Mark Eisner, trans. Alastair Reid (San Francisco: City Lights, 2004), 167.

[20] Devotional 28, Summoned. Parker J. Palmer, *Let Your Life Speak: Listening for the Voice of Vocation* (San Francisco: Jossey-Bass, 2000), 25.

[21] Devotional 29, Married to Truth. Dennis F. Kinlaw, *This Day with the Master:365 Daily Devotionals* (Grand Rapids, MI: Zondervan, 2004), January 27.

[22] Devotional 31, May the Words. Henry David Thoreau, *Walden*, ed. J. Lyndon Shanley (Princeton, NJ: Princeton University Press, 1971), 90.

[23] Devotional 33, Teaching as Annunciation. See: https://www.artsy.net/artwork/henry-ossawa-tanner-the-annunciation.

[24] Devotional 33, Teaching as Annunciation. Used by permission of the poet. "Listening for Annunciation" was first published in the December 2023 issue of the Church of the Brethren magazine, *Messenger* (Elgin, IL: Brethren Press) 19. [*Messenger* held only one-time rights.]

[25] Devotional 34, Seasons of the Soul. Allen Tate, "Seasons of the Soul," in *Collected Poems, 1919–1976* (New York: Farrar Straus Giroux, 1977), 114–22.

[26] Devotional 34, Seasons of the Soul. Christina G. Rossetti, "A Christmas Carol," *Scribner's Monthly* 3, no. 3 (New York: Scribner and Co., 1872): 278.

[27] Devotional 34, Seasons of the Soul. Mark Lowry and Buddy Greene, *Mary, Did You Know?* (Carol Stream, IL: Hope Publishing Company, 1991), recorded by Mark Lowry. To view the lyrics, visit https://www.lyrics.com/lyric/3035163/Mark%20Lowry/Mary,%20Did%20You%20Know.

[28] Devotional 37, Sneakin' in Some Sacrifice and Sacrament. Josef Pieper, *Leisure: The Basis of Culture* (South Bend, IN: St. Augustine's Press, 1998), 50.

[29] Devotional 37, Sneakin' in Some Sacrifice and Sacrament. Josef Pieper, *Leisure: The Basis of Culture* (South Bend, IN: St. Augustine's Press, 1998), 59.

[30] Devotional 38, The Double Vocation. Os Guinness, *The Call* (Nashville, TN: Thomas Nelson, 2003), 4.

[31] Devotional 38, The Double Vocation. Frederick Buechner, *Wishful Thinking* (New York: HarperOne, 1993), 95.

[32] Devotional 38, The Double Vocation. Glenn Stanton, among others, claims that Saint Francis never said or wrote this oft-repeated sentence. His argument is rather convincing, particularly since Francis never discouraged believers from verbally preaching. His writings consistently emphasized that clear proclamation

of the gospel must be demonstrated in one's everyday life, see https://www.thegospelcoalition.org/article/factchecker-misquoting-francis-of-assisi/.

[33] Devotional 39, Moral Culpability and God's Omniscience. Léon Bloy, quoted in Jacques Maritain, *Notebooks* (Albany, NY: Magi Books, 1984), 62.

[34] Devotional 40, A Prayer for Writers. Henry David Thoreau, *Walden*, ed. J. Lyndon Shanley (Princeton, NJ: Princeton University Press, 1971), 10.

[35] Devotional 41, The Saving Power of the Holy Face. Mark Altrogge, "You Sat Down," in *Songs of Fellowship: Over 600 of the Greatest Worship Songs & Hymns of Yesterday and Today* (Kingsway Music Ltd., 1995), hymn no. 639, accessed December 11, 2025, https://hymnary.org/hymnal/sof1995.

[36] Devotional 41, The Saving Power of the Holy Face. Titian, *Christ and the Good Thief*, ca. 1566, oil on canvas, 137 × 149 cm, Pinacoteca Nazionale di Bologna, Bologna, Italy. To view the painting, visit https://www.wikiart.org/en/titian/christ-and-the-good-thief.

[37] Devotional 42, Meditation on Mercy. William Shakespeare, *The Merchant of Venice*, Act 4, Scene 1, lines 1–4, *The Folger Shakespeare*, accessed September 6, 2025, https://www.folger.edu/explore/shakespeares-works/the-merchant-of-venice/read/4/1/.

[38] Devotional 43, What is Truth? Coined by Forest Long in 1972 and now used as the United Negro College Fund's slogan, see www.uncf.org.

[39] Devotional 44, The Seat of the Scornful. This is my adaptation of the King James Version to avoid gender specific language.

[40] Devotional 49, My Foolishness and God's Wisdom. J. R. R. Tolkien, *The Lord of the Rings: One Volume* (New York: Houghton Mifflin Harcourt, 2012), 589. Originally published in 1955.

[41] Devotional 51, The Work of (Y)our Hands. Unpublished poem inscribed on A. Chase Mitchell's ancestor's mug.

[42] Devotional 51, The Work of (Y)our Hands. A version of this devotional was originally published in *Christian Scholar's Review*'s "Christ Animating Learning Blog," https://christianscholars.com/ (January 6, 2022). Reprinted here with permission.

Index

people of the book, 155
Percy, Walker, 45
perseverance, 77
Peter, 183
phenomenological report, 119
phenomenology, 124
Philippians 3:14, 57
Philippians 4:6–7, 51
Philippians, 87–88
philosophical truth, 165
philosophy, 57–58, 66, 101, 123–24
   ancient, 124
   medieval, 124
Pieper, Josef, 144
Pilate, 111
Port-au-Prince, 91
Portugal, 108
potter, 197–98
prayer, 1, 4, 25, 28, 48, 52, 70, 75, 77,
   80, 119, 121, 186, 194
prayer for writers, 157
Preambles of Faith, 101
pregnancy, 24–25
Pregnancy Resource Center, 24
pride, 18
priesthood of all believers, 149
Prince, Derek, 169
   *Through the Psalms with Derek
   Prince* (book), 169
professor, 28, 31, 35–37, 39, 44,
   46–47
professors, 79–81, 84, 88, 97
   Afghan, 84
   Christian, 97
pro-life, 24
promotion and tenure, 173
Protestant, 43–46
Psalm 90:17, 199

raham, 163
Rascal Flats, 21
reconciliation, 43–44
Redeemer, 202
redemption, 28–29

refugee resettlement, 108–9
refugees, 108–9
rejection, 18
relativism, 166
religion, 43, 202
Renaissance, 159
repentant thief, 159
research paths, 201
Resignation, Great, 52
rest, 185–87
   in God, 186
   sabbath, 186
Return of the King, The (Tolkien)
   (book), 189
revelation, 111
revival, 80–81
rhema, 111
Rock (God as), 193–94
Romans 12:16, 189
Romans, 191
Rosetti, Christina, 132
rubric, 173–75

sabbath, 186
sabbatical leave, 124
sacrament, 144–45
sacrifice, 144
Sagan Society, 6
Saint-Louis, 123
Salmonella typhi, 56
salt and light, 116
salvation, 161
Sammons, Jack L., 122, 157
Sayers, Dorothy L., 45
scholarly creativity, 202
scripture, 1, 18, 99, 169
seasons of the soul, 132
seat of the scornful, 169–70
secular schools, 27
self-censoring, 32
seminary, 66, 178
Senegal, 123–24, 177–78
Senior Capstone Program, 20
sermons, 119